Living with the coast of Maine

Living with the shore

Living with the coast of Maine

Joseph T. Kelley, Alice R. Kelley, and Orrin H. Pilkey, Sr.

Sponsored by the National Audubon Society_{TM} and the Maine Geological Survey

Duke University Press   Durham and London 1989

The National Audubon Society and Its Mission

In the late 1800s, forward-thinking people became concerned over the slaughter of plumed birds for the millinery trade. They gathered together in groups to protest, calling themselves Audubon societies after the famous painter and naturalist John James Audubon. In 1905, thirty-five state Audubon groups incorporated as the National Association of Audubon Societies for the Protection of Wild Birds and Animals, since shortened to National Audubon Society. Now, with more than half a million members, five hundred chapters, ten regional offices, a twenty-five million dollar budget, and a staff of two hundred seventy-three, the Audubon Society is a powerful force for conservation, research, education, and action.

The Society's headquarters are in New York City; the legislative branch works out of an office on Capitol Hill in Washington, D.C. Ecology camps, environmental education centers, research stations, and eighty sanctuaries are strategically located around the country. The Society publishes a prize-winning magazine, *Audubon*, an ornithological journal, *American Birds*, a newspaper of environmental issues and Society activities, *Audubon Action*, and a newsletter as part of the youth education program, *Audubon Adventures*.

The Society's mission is expressed by the Audubon Cause: to conserve plants and animals and their habitats, to further the wise use of land and water, to promote rational energy strategies, to protect life from pollution, and to seek solutions to global environmental problems.

National Audubon Society 950 Third Avenue New York, New York 10022

Living with the Shore Series

Publication of the various volumes in the Living with the Shore series has been greatly assisted by the following individuals and organizations: the American Conservation Association, an anonymous Texas foundation, the Charleston Natural History Society, the Coastal Zone Management Agency (NOAA), the Geraldine R. Dodge Foundation, the William H. Donner Foundation, Inc., the Federal Emergency Management Agency, the George Gund Foundation, the Mobil Oil Corporation, Elizabeth O'Connor, the Sapelo Island Research Foundation, the Sea Grant programs in New Jersey, North Carolina, Florida, Mississippi/Alabama, and New York, The Fund for New Jersey, M. Harvey Weil, and Patrick H. Welder, Jr. The Living with the Shore series is a product of the Duke University Program for the Study of Developed Shorelines, which is funded by the Donner Foundation.

© 1989 Duke University Press, all rights reserved
Printed in the United States of America on acid-free paper ∞
Library of Congress Cataloging-in-Publication Data
Kelley, Joseph T.
Living with the Main shore/by Joseph T. Kelley and Alice R. Kelley.
p. cm.—(Living with the shore)   Bibliography: p.   Includes index.
ISBN 0-8223-0864-9. ISBN 0-8223-0885-1 (pbk.)
1. Shore protection—Maine.   2. Coastal zone management—Maine.
3. Coasts—Maine   4. House construction—Maine.   I. Kelley, Alice
R.   II. Title.   III. Series.
TC224.M2K45   1989   333.91′7′09741—dc 19   88-10845

Contents

Figures and tables

Figures

Table

Acknowledgments

We wish to primarily acknowledge our parents for instilling in each
of us many of the interests and values embodied in this book.
We are especially grateful to Walter A. Anderson, of the Maine
Geological Survey, and Richard B. Anderson, former Commis-
sioner of the Maine Department of Conservation, for bringing us to
Maine in the first place. We have benefited from many discussions
with other geologists and would like to thank Daniel F. Belknap,
R. Craig Shipp, Stephen M. Dickson, Woodrow B. Thompson,
Harold W. Borns, Jr., Marcel Moreau, and Barry Timson for ad-
vancing our understanding of the coast. Finally, we thank Donald
Witherill, Teco Brown, Fred Michaud, Cheryl Ring, Ginger Davis,
Nancy Anderson, Karin Tilberg, Karen Massey, and Alison Rieser,
a group of enlightened nongeologists who, in one way or another,
have partly educated us and helped to protect Maine's coast.

Author's preface

How now my insulated friend,
What calm composure can defend your rock,
When tides the size you've never seen
Wash out the sands of what has been,
And from your island's tallest tree
You watch advance what is to be,
The tidal wave devours the shore,
There are no islands anymore.
                              —Edna St. Vincent Millay

Last August I participated in a NATO-sponsored field trip around the Bay of Fundy for a large international group of coastal scientists interested in the response of shorelines to the rising level of the sea. As I walked across the vast, flat salt marshes surrounding old Fort Beausejour, New Brunswick, the leader of the trip leaned over to me and shouted above the strong wind: "This is a horrible place for a salt marsh."

I found his statement incredible. He had just finished explaining to the 75 marine scientists from all over the world that this was the thickest salt marsh peat deposit in the region. For 6,000 years the marsh had grown upward at a rate exactly matching the rise of sea level, maintaining its surface at just the high water level. Today the marsh's history is easily examined because it is eroding, and well exposed, on its seaward margin. About three feet beneath the present marsh surface logs from a 17th-century corduroy road built by Acadians stick out of the peat and are regularly inundated by high tide. During the extremely low tides which occur at the head of the Bay of Fundy, one can see the base of the salt marsh peat resting on logs from an ancient, drowned forest. While the field trip leader was close to the mark in observing that this salt marsh is rapidly eroding, I was amazed at how he could consider any site which hosted a healthy, growing salt marsh for 6,000 years "horrible" for a marsh. While our group reached no consensus on why this marsh, and others like it, were eroding, it was clear to us that coastal conditions had profoundly changed. The suspicion lingering in most minds was that the rising level of the sea had claimed another victim. As one scientist noted: "We are losing 50 square miles of salt marsh per year in Louisiana due to rising ocean waters. Why can't it happen here?"

Indeed, although I once found it inconceivable, the worst of coastal tragedies, a conflict between rising sea level and coastal development can happen in Maine, and has already begun. As a professional geologist I have long been aware that sea level is slowly rising and drowning our coast. In the 1970s I conducted my Ph.D. research in southern New Jersey and saw at close range the worst sorts of coastal construction. I found a black humor in the plight of residents in Cape May, New Jersey, who lost poorly sited, but fabulously expensive properties to the changing shoreline. As a native of Maine's relatively wild and undeveloped coast, I could not comprehend the mentality or the motives of developers who constructed high-rise buildings so near to the margin of the sea. As a nonresident, however, I was satisfied that New Jersey's problems were no business of mine.

I lived and taught for several years in Louisiana, and only then became aware of the extraordinary economic and environmental cost to the public of unrestricted, unplanned development too close to a rising sea. It was then—and still is—mind-boggling to think of quarrying rocks in Arkansas, barging them down the Mississippi River, and using them to construct a seawall around a small but beautiful barrier island in an effort to "stabilize" it. The rocks are still there, albeit underwater, but the beauty and the beach are long since gone, and the public is stuck with the tab for cleanup. My wife and I were so stunned by the destruction caused to the Louisiana coast in an effort to develop and hold it that we wrote a book on how to live safely with that shoreline (*Living with the Louisiana Shore*, 1984).

Upon returning to Maine in 1982 I found that much of what I had once enjoyed most about the Maine coast—extensive areas of pristine, accessible shore—were no more. The worst sort of coastal development activity I had seen in New Jersey and Louisiana, including the erection of high-rise condominiums on the beach, the crowding of private residences along small barrier spits, and the wholesale walling-up of long stretches of the shoreline to hold back the sea, were already under way in Maine. I am proud to say that along with a number of other concerned people I helped win support for progressive regulations that restrict unsound development along the Maine coast. This book was written in an effort to describe the geology of Maine's coast, and in doing so to justify the restrictions we place on coastal zone construction here. I would like my children to have the same opportunity to grow up along a beautiful coastline as I once had, but I am no longer so naive as to believe that such good things simply happen without effort. The continued need for educating the public about coastal processes and shoreline change is my purpose in writing this book, and the reason for it recently came back to me at a public hearing in southern Maine. I had just testified to the Board of Environmental Protection in favor of regulations that preclude the construction of new seawalls and the enlargement of existing ones along our coast. A woman who summers in Wells, Maine, strenuously objected to my comments and approached me after the hearing. "Who needs the beach anyway?" she exclaimed. "The sand just gets tracked onto the carpet and makes a mess. Besides, I love the sound of waves crashing into the seawall at night."

This book is dedicated to those people who understand the value of "mountains without hand rails," and beaches without seawalls!

Joseph T. Kelley
April 24, 1988
Orono, Maine

Editors' preface

The Maine book is the second "Living with the Shore" volume to be written and compiled by Joe and Alice Kelley. A few years back Joe taught at the University of New Orleans, and he and Alice produced *Living with the Louisiana Shore*. Clearly, Joe's Maine accent was out of place in the Mississippi Delta, so back the couple came to the northeast where they soon took up the task of writing *Living with the Coast of Maine*. The work is a labor of love, as the Kelleys, like all of the authors in the series, receive only thanks and perhaps some satisfaction as payment for their long hours of effort.

With the publication of *Living with the Coast of Maine*, the series now boasts 15 books, all of which are listed on the inside cover of this volume. *The Beaches Are Moving* by Wallace Kaufman and Orrin H. Pilkey, Jr., which recently was reprinted for the third time by Duke University Press, is the important "umbrella" volume for the series.

The overall coastal book project is an outgrowth of initial support from the National Oceanic and Atmospheric Administration (NOAA) through the Office of Coastal Zone Management. The initial project was administered through the North Carolina Sea Grant Program. More recently it has been generously supported by the Federal Emergency Management Agency (FEMA). Without FEMA support the series would not have proceeded this far. However, the conclusions presented herein are those of the authors and do not necessarily represent those of the supporting agencies.

We owe a debt of gratitude to many individuals for support, ideas, encouragement, and information. Doris Schroeder has helped us in many ways as Jill-of-all-trades over a span of more than a decade and more than a dozen books. The Duke University Press staff compiled the index for this volume. The original idea for a coastal book (*How to Live with an Island* [1972]) was that of Pete Chenery, then director of the North Carolina Science and Technology Center. Richard Foster of the Federal Coastal Zone Management Agency supported the project at a critical juncture. Because of his lifelong commitment to land conservation, Richard Pough, former head of The Nature Conservancy, has been a mainstay in our fund-raising efforts. Myrna Jackson of the Duke University Development Office has been most helpful in our search for financial support.

Jane Bullock of the Federal Emergency Management Agency has been a constant source of assistance and encouragement as she has helped us chart a course through the shifting channels of the federal government. Richard Krimm, Peter Gibson, Dennis Carroll, Jim Collins, Jet Battley, Melita Rodeck, Chris Makris, and many others have opened doors, provided maps, charts, and publications, and generally helped us through the Washington maze.

As with any effort of this sort, we were helped by many people who live and work by the shore, so many we cannot begin to list them all. We are grateful for their cooperation, insight, and concern.

Last but not least, we extend our thanks to Lynne Claflin, Virginia Henderson, and Tonya Clayton for doing a lot of the drafting and manuscript/figure preparation.

We dedicate this work to all those who helped us and to all who enjoy the beautiful shoreline of Maine.

Orrin H. Pilkey, Jr.
William J. Neal
Series editors

1 A coastal perspective

Along the East and Gulf coasts of the United States, barrier islands protecting extensive salt marshes and bays are the most common sort of shoreline environments. In almost all locations the barrier islands are moving landward in response to the world's rising sea level. While geologists accept the landward migration of sandy barrier islands and muddy salt marshes as a natural and important process, the recreation-minded public usually does not. For many years developers have constructed residences and businesses on barrier islands; indeed, modern cities exist on some barriers, and the owners of these structures equate beach movement with erosion and disaster. Developers and homeowners frequently enlist the aid of engineers to construct shore protection structures to hold back the sea. The first coastal region to undergo such massive and rapid development gave rise to the term "New Jerseyization," referring to a similar pattern of construction taking place in many coastal areas today. In other places conservationists and the inexorable forces of nature have prevailed, and former settlements have been abandoned. Some of these areas are now our national seashores and national wildlife sanctuaries.

The coast of Maine is markedly different from the region south of Cape Cod (fig. 1.1). Repeated glaciations during the Ice Ages of the past 2 million years removed the flat Coastal Plain materi-

als common in the southeastern United States, leaving a rocky and highly irregular coast. Although there are barrier beaches in Maine, they are scarce and usually tied to rocky headlands. Similarly, while Maine possesses extensive salt marshes, mud flats are the single most common coastal setting in the state (fig. 1.2). Partly as a result of these geographic differences, and possibly because Maine's refreshing ocean water is considered too cold by those from the south, the widespread development apparent in New Jersey or Florida is less common in Maine. Nevertheless, there are beach communities with the first growing pains of New Jerseyization already apparent (fig. 1.3). In addition, Maine possesses many high bluffs of landslide-prone Ice Age mud which are attracting the attention of unwary developers. Thus the beaches and bluffs of Maine's "soft coast," which were avoided by the ever-cautious pioneering Yankees who originally settled on the bedrock promontories of the state, are attracting a new class of recreation-oriented coastal developers (fig. 1.4).

Although the coastal regions of Maine were the original locations of settlement and have long been popular sites for resorts, unprecedented numbers of people have moved into Maine's coastal zone or visited it since 1950 (fig. 1.5). A disproportionate number of tourists reached only York and Cumberland counties, where most of the sand beaches are located. Along with residences and businesses, the infrastructure of sewers, services, and the roads they require are beginning to crowd themselves onto Maine's tidally influenced shoreline (fig. 1.3). Independent of this human tide moving toward the ocean, the Maine coast is changing in re-

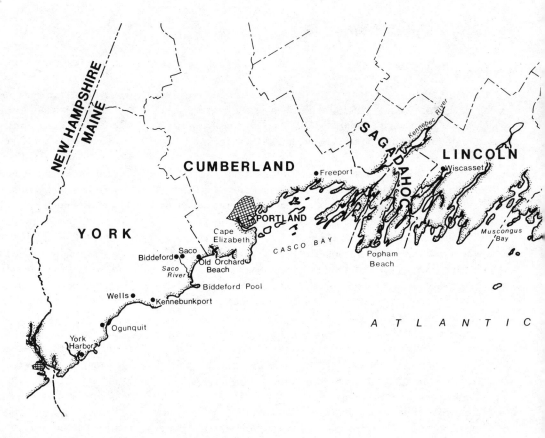

Figure 1.1. Index map of the coast of Maine.

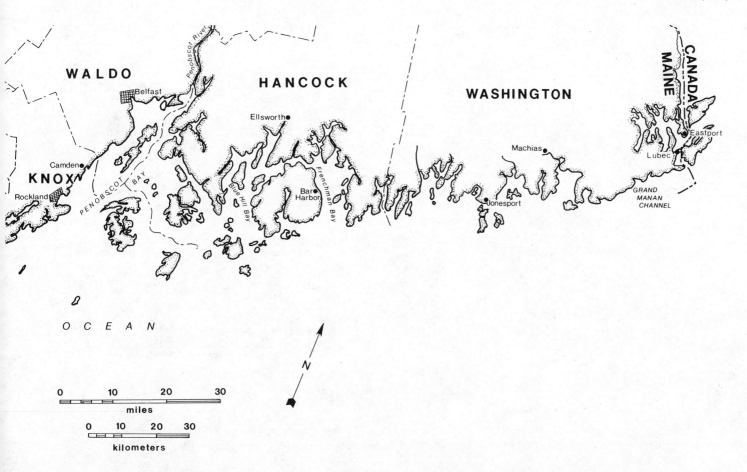

WALDO

HANCOCK

WASHINGTON

CANADA

MAINE

Penobscot River

Belfast

Ellsworth

Eastport

Camden

Machias

Lubec

KNOX

Bar
Harbor

Jonesport

GRAND
MANAN
CHANNEL

Rockland

Frenchman Bay

Blue Hill Bay

PENOBSCOT BAY

OCEAN

N

0	10	20	30

miles

0	10	20	30

kilometers

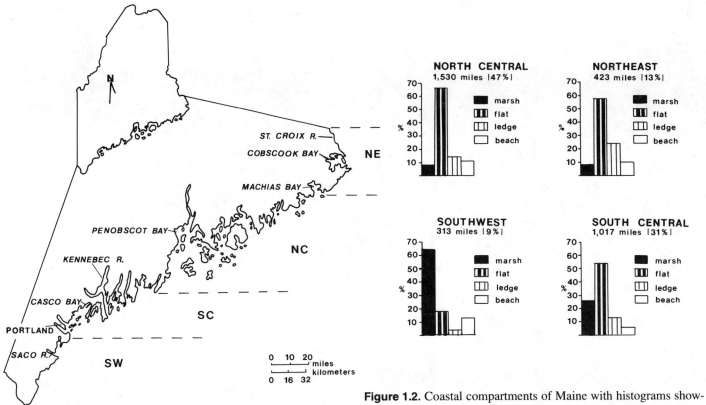

Figure 1.2. Coastal compartments of Maine with histograms showing the length of each compartment's tidal shoreline and estimated proportion of various environments.

A

B

Figure 1.3. Incipient "New Jerseyization" in coastal Maine: (a) Old Orchard Beach (b) Short Sands Beach, York.

sponse to land and sea movements. The southern and northern coastal regions are sinking relatively rapidly and experiencing earthquakes and landslides in conjunction with their movement. While some beaches in Maine have disappeared within recorded history, others have appeared. Uniformly along the coast, bluffs erode at rates of 1 to 3 feet per year (fig. 1.4). In addition to this natural change, plans are being seriously discussed to dam part of the Bay of Fundy in nearby Canada. This tidal power dam is expected to cause 6-inch higher and 6-inch lower tides, which will have an extraordinary impact on Maine's shoreline. This book describes the recent geologic and cultural history of the Maine coast and compares it with other regions of the United States. It provides recommendations on where to live and how to live safely with change.

History of development

Settlement began along the Maine coast prior to that of any other area of the United States. There are records of temporary fishing communities on Maine islands as long ago as the sixteenth century. Before that, Native American Indians "summered" at many of today's popular beaches. A nineteenth-century historian noted: "This [Camp Ellis] was a favorite resort for the early Indian tribes. . . . Here at the mouth of the Saco [River], in view of the bright island in the bay, the tribes came to feast upon the seabirds and shellfish so abundant at this shore."

The impact of these early activities was minimal. It was not

B

Figure 1.4. Bluff erosion and stabilization in Jonesport: (a) April 1983 and (b) April 1987.

until the early nineteenth century that development along the coast began to be noticeable. The year Maine gained statehood, 1820, saw the first beach resort at Old Orchard. William Scammon's "Camp Comfort" provided lodging for visitors to what was then a pristine barrier beach. As a precursor to today's Old Orchard Beach amusement park, however, Camp Comfort also housed a bowling alley.

This early establishment was an extension of a private home and more akin to a modern bed-and-breakfast inn than a resort. By 1900, however, a railroad line had been constructed to bring in masses of tourists, and 25 grand hotels and more than 800 summer cottages annually accommodated 200,000 visitors with beds for more than 12,000 people per night. Similarly at York Beach, Maine, development increased from the first hotel in 1869 to more than 500 beach houses in 1929. In 1889 the state's first amusement ride, a "marine car" which rode rails over the sea, was built at York Beach.

As today's major coastal tourist attractions were beginning to form at Old Orchard, York, and Popham beaches, another kind of development was occurring. Economic expansion in Maine and other northeastern states promoted a growing class of wealthy families who sought to leave the cities in the summer. Through the late nineteenth and early twentieth centuries summer "cottages" began to appear at numerous scenic, rocky promontories overlooking the sea (fig. 1.6). At first these were intermingled with fishermen's shacks, but after a time cottage communities dominated places like Perkins Cove, Prouts Neck, Cape Elizabeth, and Bar Harbor. Although these communities represented intense development along specific rocky cliffs, the popular spots were widely separated, and in the case of Mount Desert Island accessible only by boat.

Since World War II an increase in private car ownership, more extensive networks of roads and bridges, and more regular ferry service to the islands have led to a profound increase in coastal popularity and development (fig. 1.5). Spreading as a wave from the New Hampshire border, residences have appeared not only on every available space of large beaches like Old Orchard but also on smaller, frequently less stable strandlines. Similarly, following development of the most scenic rocky overlooks, construction is increasingly common on the eroding bluffs of glacial sediment along the coast.

Because of the great size of its coast and distance from population centers, Maine seldom worried and usually encouraged coastal development. In many areas, however, coastal growth has gotten out of hand. The property owners of Moody Beach in southern Maine recently sued the town to prevent the public from walking on the intertidal beach. Old Orchard, the crown jewel of Maine's sand beaches, is showing the first conspicuous signs of New Jerseyization. Severe beach erosion adjacent to U.S. Army Corps of Engineers' stabilization structures mark the inlets at each end of the beach, while high-rise condominiums have been erected on the former dunes of this once beautiful beach. Most recently, the town located its sewer pipes under the beach and dunes.

A trip to the coasts of New Jersey or Massachusetts would be

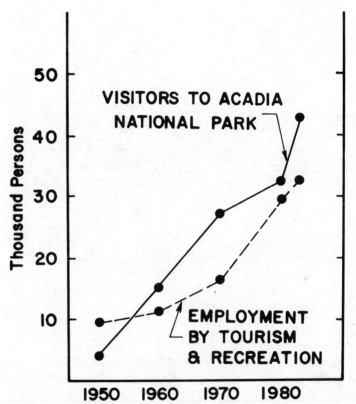

Figure 1.5. Maine's increasing tourist business, 1950 to 1980. (Modified from *The Economy of Maine*, September 1985, University of Southern Maine, Center for Research and Advanced Study.)

Figure 1.6. Crowded cottage development near Cape Neddick.

Figure 1.7. Total coast development at Winthrop, Massachusetts. Note that the original sources of sand—the eroding bluffs in the foreground and background—are riprapped to protect a water tower and condominiums, respectively. The original beach, long eroded, has been nourished to the edge of its massive seawall and is protected by a series of offshore breakwaters.

worthwhile for every Mainer (fig. 1.7). The sight of their developed shorelines conveys a more dramatic message than the pages of any book. New Jerseyization destroys natural beauty, and yet beauty is in the eye of the beholder; some people prefer a hot dog stand on the beach to a dune covered with beach grass. There are, however, nonaesthetic problems of New Jerseyization that pose a more serious threat to coastal residents.

Storms

Few of the state's summer visitors directly witness the storms that have the greatest impact on Maine's coast (fig. 1.8). Unlike

Figure 1.8. Seawall at Silver Sands Hotel during February 1978 storm. Photo by John Patriquin and Jim Daniels, *Portland Press Herald*.

Figure 1.9. Wreckage of Old Orchard Beach pier following the February 1978 storm. Photo by Peter Darling, *Maine Sunday Telegram*.

most other locations along the U.S. East Coast, Maine's most damaging storms occur in winter. Often called northeasters or southwesters, after the direction from which the wind blows most strongly, Maine's winter storms may reach hurricane proportions and last for days. Prior to recent large-scale development of sand beaches and other coastal lowlands, winter blizzards were noted for their snowfalls or shipwrecks. Present-day winter storms are now characterized by the dollar amount of property damage. The January and February storms of 1978 are renowned for causing an estimated $47 million in damage to coastal structures (fig. 1.9). While few lives are lost during storms today because of timely warnings from the National Weather Service, the price of future winter storms is certain to increase (see appendix A).

Pollution

Improper waste disposal threatens the health of coastal citizens and destroys the natural resources that support the local marine fishing industry. In North Carolina 20 percent of the estuarine fishing grounds for clams, oysters, shrimp, and fish have already been closed because of pollution. In Maine 33 percent of the mud flats and salt marshes are closed to the taking of shellfish due to pollution. Despite progressive laws that restrict the disposal of raw sewage, many inhabitants of the islands and rocky peninsulas of central Maine with insufficient soil for septic systems use "overboard disposal" via outfall pipes from private homes (fig. 1.10). Attempts to construct large, environmentally damaging oil refineries or power plants have been defeated in Casco, Penobscot, and Cobscook bays, but the specter of industrialization similar to that of northern New Jersey lingers over the economically underdeveloped coast of Maine. Sears Island, in Penobscot Bay, has recently been selected as the site of a major port facility, and a 2,000 megawatt coal-fired power plant is being discussed for Cobscook Bay.

Environmental destruction

The beach, the very environment we rush to the coast to enjoy, is ultimately destroyed when it is overdeveloped (fig. 1.11). Scenic dunes, maritime forests, and marsh habitats gradually disappear under the roads, parking lots, and foundations of buildings. This alteration of the environment is the most striking aspect of New Jerseyization. Beach and property-saving structures work only temporarily at best. Where seawalls are built the beach is eventually lost. Old beach resorts in Florida, Virginia, and New Jersey have

Figure 1.10. Sewage disposal pipe crossing beach near Biddeford Pool.

no beaches at all except where sand has been pumped in. In addition, beach repair costs the taxpayer a great deal of money. Miami Beach's latest beach restoration project, begun in 1977, will erode the public coffers by $89 million.

Reduced public access

Private development on the coast inevitably reduces public access to the beach or scenic rocky overlooks (fig. 1.12). Yet the shoreline, particularly the beach, has traditionally been an area for all the public to enjoy. When eroding beaches require sand replenishment or marinas need sand removal, the public is asked to pay for it. Similarly, when storms destroy coastal properties, public-supported federal flood insurance rescues homeowners. Many beaches are off-limits to the same public, however, because no parking is permitted within miles of the beach or because the road to the beach is privately owned, in part, and blocked by a gate. In southern Maine beachfront homeowners are seeking to exclude the public who do reach the beach from crossing in front of their properties. Maine, which has one of the longest and most scenic shorelines in the United States, also has the most privately owned, least accessible coast (fig. 5.1). With the growing number of summer visitors as well as residents who feel they have a right to enjoy the coast, public access to Maine's shoreline is a problem reaching crisis proportions.

A

B

Figure 1.11. (a) Back dune environment along a developed beach (Wells) and (b) undeveloped dune (Ferry Beach State Park).

Figure 1.12. No public access is possible along (a) the Prouts Neck coast or (b) some beaches in the Kennebunk area.

Coastal calamities: a stormy past

As mentioned previously, the earliest non-native development of the Maine coast appears to have been seasonal fishing camps. The more permanent occupation of the coast brought more structures to the water's edge. However, these buildings were usually restricted to the business at hand—warehouses, fish houses, wharves, and the like. Homes were still wisely placed well above the tide line and frequently on rocky headlands or high ground. With this development "plan," severe storms might be an economic hardship to the fisherman and merchant who were located at the water's edge, but few people lost their homes to the raging surf.

The 21 March 1876 edition of the *Portland Eastern Argus* carried an article detailing the damage done to the Old Orchard House by a southeasterly storm. The building, which was under construction, was to have been one of the largest hotels on the coast. The reporter termed the structure "demolished." This hotel was just one of a long line of poorly sited structures that have been lost to storms.

As the nineteenth century drew to a close, more and more accounts of storm damage appear in the press. Damage to hotels, cottages, and amusement piers became more frequent as the recreational development of the coast escalated. In 1896 the famous Old Orchard Beach Pier did not survive even one year unscathed. Built in the spring, the pier collapsed during a November northeaster.

More recently, a quartet of storms in the 1970s has served to remind coastal residents of the Atlantic's winter fury. In 1972 a February storm did over $1.5 million in damage, primarily in southern coastal Maine. The Old Orchard Beach Pier was damaged in the storm. The *York County Coast Star*, 23 February 1972, predicted that the pier would "rise like Venus from the waves." A spring storm in March of 1976 toppled Popham Beach cottages into the ocean, at an estimated cost of $2 million (fig. 1.13). The same storm was responsible for extensive damage to roads in the Camp Ellis section of Saco. The Old Orchard Beach Pier which rose like Venus from the 1972 storm fell in the face of a pair of storms in 1978 (fig. 1.14). The first storm hit on 9 January 1978, damaging homes and businesses in southern and central coastal Maine. The second storm, the stronger of the two, hit a month

Figure 1.14. Destruction of the Old Orchard Beach pier during a 1972 storm. Photo by Peter Darling, *Maine Sunday Telegram*.

Figure 1.13. Property damage following beach erosion at Popham Beach in 1976.

later on 8 February. Pieces of the Old Orchard Beach Pier were found in the town's business section. Homes, businesses, and seawalls, many freshly repaired from the January storm, fell in the face of the February onslaught. The cost of damages for the two storms totaled $47 million.

If the same storm were to hit today, the price would certainly be higher, as more and more people flock to the Maine coast. Although some people consider storms to be rare "acts of God," in fact they are regular and predictable events in this region (fig. 1.15). While the number of storms differs from year to year, hardly a winter goes by without a major northeaster.

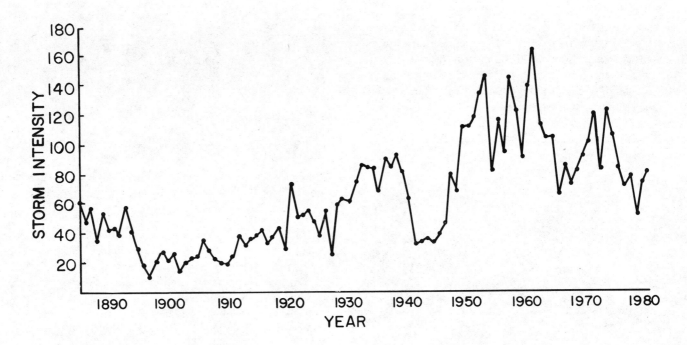

Figure 1.15. Graph showing storm intensity for Cape Cod, Massachusetts, since the nineteenth century. (Modified from Aubrey and Speer, 1983.)

2 Maine's changing coastline

Geologic history of the Maine coast

The tourist brochures extol the virtues of Maine's "rockbound coast" and "timeless sand beaches." For the summer visitor at Acadia National Park or Reid Beach State Park these probably seem like appropriate descriptions. Maine's coast has many more environments than sand beaches and rocky cliffs, however, and has changed more in the past few thousand years than any other place along the U.S. East Coast. The reasons behind the popular misconception are the extreme length of Maine's shoreline and its general inaccessibility and lack of previous study.

If one traces a straight line from the Maine/New Hampshire state line to the Canadian border, the distance is about 250 miles. The coastline is highly irregular, however, and includes so many islands that the state's "tidal shoreline," or length of coast influenced by tides, is about 3,500 miles. Although the most popular places along this coast are a handful of high rocky cliffs and sandy beaches, careful observation shows that mud flats and salt marshes are among the most common coastal settings (fig. 1.2). To appreciate the configuration of the present coastline and better anticipate future changes, it is essential to understand its past. The geological history of coastal Maine may be conveniently divided into five time periods of very different lengths.

Bedrock formation

Unlike the states south of New York City, Maine has ancient bedrock exposed along its coast. The bedrock of coastal Maine (fig. 2.1) is very complicated and originated many hundred million years ago as a vast accumulation of sand and mud along the margin of a youthful North America. Beginning about 420 million years ago and continuing through about 320 million years ago, these sand and mud layers were caught in a continental collision involving Europe and North America and were squeezed into mountains. The accompanying heat of this upheaval transformed the sand and mud into metamorphic rocks, which today surround formerly molten granite masses. Following this, hundreds of millions of years of erosion have removed the mountains and left hills where granitic rocks have been worn down relatively slowly, and valleys where more easily eroded metamorphic rocks have been preferentially eroded.

On the basis of the bedrock geology, it is appropriate to subdivide the coast into four compartments (fig. 1.2). The *arcuate embayments compartment* forms the southwestern coast of Maine. It comprises exposures of granitic or crystalline rock that, because of their resistance to erosion, form high headlands such as Cape Neddick. Between the resistant headlands are arcuate bays with extensive salt marshes and sand beaches. Most of the sand beaches in Maine exist between Saco and Wells bays (fig. 2.2).

From Portland to Penobscot Bay stretches the *indented shoreline compartment*. Glaciers have scraped deep valleys out of the soft metamorphic rocks of this region to form long, narrow estuaries

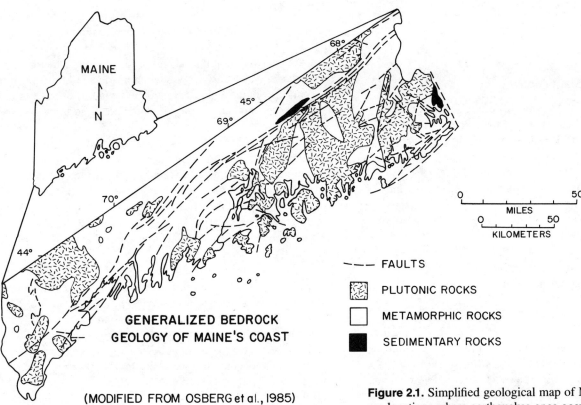

MAINE

N

68°

45°

69°

70°

44°

GENERALIZED BEDROCK
GEOLOGY OF MAINE'S COAST

(MODIFIED FROM OSBERG et al., 1985)

0   50
MILES
0   50
KILOMETERS

–·–·– FAULTS

PLUTONIC ROCKS

METAMORPHIC ROCKS

SEDIMENTARY ROCKS

Figure 2.1. Simplified geological map of Maine's coast. The faults are locations where earthquakes once occurred during ancient rock movements. (Modified from Osberg, Hussey, and Boone, 1985.)

Figure 2.2. The Arcuate Embayments Compartment is composed of sand beaches and salt marshes in regions that are punctuated by occasional rocky headlands as in this photo of the Kennebunk area.

separated by peninsulas. Mud flats are the most common environments along this coast, and sand beaches are well developed only at the mouth of the Kennebec River (fig. 2.3).

The area from Penobscot Bay to Machias Bay is referred to as the *island-bay complex* and is the longest compartment on the Maine coast. It is composed of erosion-resistant islands of granitic bedrock, such as Mount Desert Island, in broad embayments carved out of metamorphic rock. Sand beaches in this area are

rare, although small cobble beaches are common. Sand Beach in Acadia National Park is a unique beach within this compartment and is composed largely of broken seashells rather than the more familiar quartz sand (fig. 2.4).

The northern *cliffed shoreline compartment* in Maine is remote and rarely seen by summer visitors. Its high cliffs of volcanic rock do not permit any sandy beaches, and only to the north, on the St. Croix River estuary, are such features found (fig. 2.5). Fortunately, there are few developed beaches in this area. Recent

Figure 2.3. The Indented Shoreline Compartment's narrow estuaries shelter numerous small salt marshes and mud flats.

Figure 2.4. Sand beach in Acadia National Park is unusual in this rocky compartment because it consists mostly of broken seashells.

geological research indicates that it is an area of rapid subsidence and earthquakes.

Most recent Ice Age

During the past several million years there have been repeated advances and retreats of the world's glaciers due to profound changes in the earth's climate. The most recent glacial advance involved ice moving from the Hudson Bay region across New England as far south as Cape Cod and Long Island. In fact, Long

Island and Cape Cod are composed largely of till deposits, or sand, mud, and boulders left by the ice. Their position marks the maximum extent of the most recent Ice Age, about 20,000 years ago (fig. 2.6).

Melting ice reached the Maine coast about 13,000 years ago. One important effect of the Ice Age was to remove any soils that existed prior to the glaciation. This is why Maine has so much exposed rock. The preglacial soils, along with copious amounts of broken-up rock, were transported and left by the ice as till deposits, which often form conspicuous hills in the coastal area. Great Hill in Kennebunk and the eroding bluffs near Rogue Bluffs

Figure 2.5. Much of the Cliffed Shoreline Compartment is still dominated by an undeveloped rocky coastline.

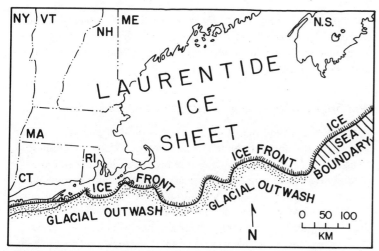

Figure 2.6. New England at the peak of the Ice Age. (Modified from J. Schlee and R. M. Pratt, *Atlantic Continental Shelf and Slope of the United States*, 1970, U.S. Geological Survey, Professional Paper 529-H).

State Park are only two of many glacial deposits left along Maine's coast (fig. 2.7).

Postglacial drowning of coastal Maine

The glacier that covered Maine's highest mountains weighed so much that it depressed, or squeezed down, the rocky crust of the earth beneath it. As the ice melted away about 12,500 years ago, the ocean flooded the lowered coastal areas and major river valleys like the Kennebec and Penobscot (fig. 2.8). While the ocean waters covered the state, rock flour, or glacially ground-up rocks, began to accumulate on the new seafloor. This marine mud, which besides seashells occasionally contains boulders dropped by icebergs, is called the *Presumpscot Formation*. It is named after the Presumpscot River, in Cumberland County, which has banks

Figure 2.7. Erosion of glacial deposits, like the spectacular bluff at Great Hill, Kennebunk, has provided the sand for beaches in regions lacking a major river.

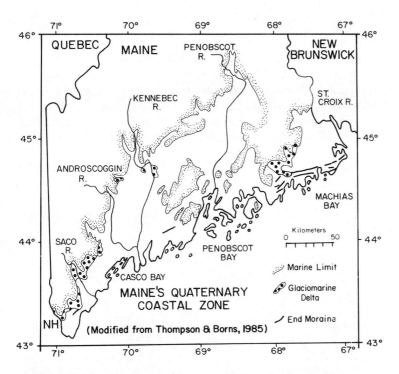

Figure 2.8. The Quaternary, or Ice Age, features of coastal Maine. Moraines are large hills of sand and gravel left by the ice. The glaciomarine deltas formed 12,500 years ago when the shoreline was at the marine limit, a considerable distance from the present coast. (Modified from Thompson and Borns, 1985.)

piled high with the mud. At the time of greatest drowning, great deltas of sand were left by the melting ice. These are the blueberry barrens near Cherryfield (fig. 2.8) and sandy plains near Sanford and Sebago Lake today.

Withdrawal of the sea and emergence of the land

After the ice melted out of the mountains of Maine around 11,500 years ago, the land rebounded to its former elevation. The sea retreated from the land so quickly that few shorelines cut into the glacial deposits during this period are known today. As the land became emergent, the former seafloor mud, the Presumpscot Formation, became unstable. It slumped to fill old river valleys. Thus hilly areas lost their sediment cover and bare rock was exposed. In the lowlands, new rivers were unable to relocate their old channels, which were buried by glacial till and marine deposits. Thus waterfalls became common even near the coast. We do not know when the land stopped emerging from the ocean, but recent marine geologic research shows a prominent shoreline off the coast at 200 feet below sea level. This marks the lowest recent location of sea level from about 9,500 years ago.

Modern drowning of the coast

After the land stopped rising due to removal of the ice, continued worldwide melting of glaciers caused the level of the sea to rise. It continues to rise up to the present (fig. 2.9), although not at

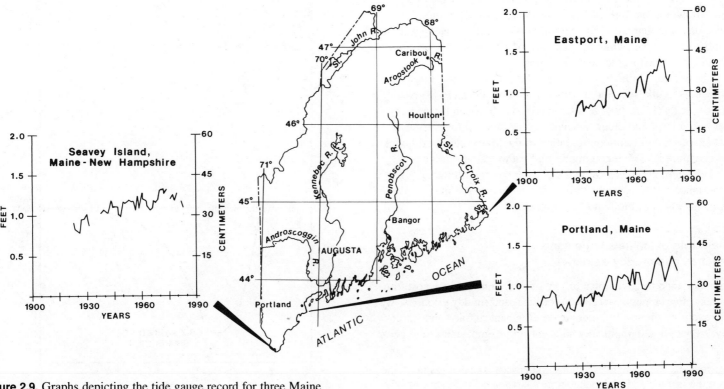

Figure 2.9. Graphs depicting the tide gauge record for three Maine cities. The rate of sea-level rise is greatest in the Eastport area where the land is also sinking.

a uniform rate. Downeast (northeast coastal) Maine shows very rapid drowning because of land subsidence possibly related to earthquakes in that area. The central portion of the coast appears to be relatively stable, while the southern portion is slowly subsiding, though not as fast as the northern coast.

Thus coastal Maine has experienced a glaciation, two coastal drownings by the sea, and a withdrawal of the ocean in the past 14,000 years (fig. 2.10). It is the interaction between the ongoing rise in sea level and older, glacial, marine, and bedrock materials that shapes the present configuration of the Maine coast. Although the coastline is evolving along myriad pathways depending on the local geology, there are two changing coastal settings of great importance to the coastal resident: barrier beach/salt marsh environments and soft bluff/mud flat regions.

The origin of Maine's large sand beaches and muddy estuaries

To understand the dynamics of two of the Maine coast's most important environments, large sand beaches and muddy estuaries, we will examine the recent geologic development of Saco and Casco bays. Though geographically adjacent, these embayments are geo-

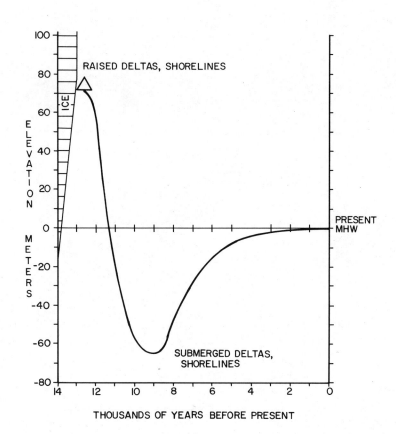

Figure 2.10. The changing relationship between land and sea in Maine since the last Ice Age. Note that large coastal areas were covered by the sea about 12,000 years ago, then emerged by 9,000 years ago. (Modified from Belknap and others, 1987.)

logically quite different. Saco Bay is in the arcuate embayments compartment of the coast (fig. 1.2). It is dominated by a large sand beach, Old Orchard Beach, which is bounded by two rocky headlands: Prouts Neck to the north and Biddeford Pool to the south (fig. 2.11). Old Orchard Beach is an important recreational area, which attracts visitors from both the United States and Canada. The town of Old Orchard Beach as well as neighboring communities have undergone a burst of development in the last 20 years, much of it concentrated directly on the coast.

Casco Bay to the north is part of the indented shoreline compartment of the coast. It extends from Cape Elizabeth northward to Harpswell Neck and is typified by long, narrow estuaries separated by peninsulas (fig. 2.11). With the economic growth of southern Maine, the Casco Bay area has been the site of increasing commercial and residential development. Year-round and recreational homes are increasing in the coastal area—many of them on the "soft" bluffs facing the bay's estuaries.

Saco Bay—large sand beaches

Beaches are often called dynamic or changing environments. In Maine the amount of change beaches have undergone is extreme. Using Old Orchard Beach in Saco Bay as an example, we will consider the processes that have shaped that strandline and others like it.

About 9,000 years ago the Saco River delivered large quantities of sand from eroded glacial deposits in the mountains to a location

Figure 2.11. The present coast of Casco and Saco bays.

about 10 miles off the present coast (fig. 2.12) and at a present depth of 200 feet. Waves reworked this river sediment into a long barrier spit by a process called *longshore drift* (fig. 2.13). Since the prevailing winds were probably the same then as now, the barrier probably grew in the direction the wind blew, from southwest to northeast. Here and there, eroding outcrops of glacial material contributed more sand or gravel to the beach, and occasional rock ledges may have intercepted the flow. Inlets, or breaches in the spit, probably existed where small rivers like the Scarborough and Spurwink reached the coast.

At the time of this early beach's formation a forest occupied much of Saco Bay and small salt marshes rimmed the margins of the estuarine rivers. Large winter storms occasionally swept across the ocean-facing beach and moved large quantities of sand from the ocean side to the estuarine side as an overwash deposit (fig. 2.14). Thus as sea level rose the barrier beach was maintained by daily contributions of river sand, which was dispersed by wave action. In the years between major storms, the wind blew sand into dunes, which acted as sand reservoirs when stabilized by plants. When a storm came, the sand was washed landward and the daily

Figure 2.12. The coast of Casco and Saco bays approximately 9,000 years ago when sea level was about 200 feet lower than today. The stippled area represents the present-day shoreline. (Based on oceanographic research described in a paper by Kelley, Kelley, Shipp, and Belknap, 1986.)

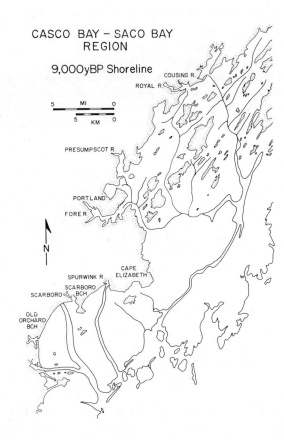

CASCO BAY – SACO BAY
REGION

9,000yBP Shoreline

processes repeated themselves, although at a higher and more landward location than before.

By 6,000 years ago the processes of sand introduction by rivers and eroding bluffs, and sand dispersal by waves, winds, and storms, had permitted the Saco Bay beach systems to migrate several miles landward to a present depth of about 60 feet (fig. 2.15). The great speed at which the sea rose resulted in the drowning of some beaches that were bordered by rocks in the Bluff Island area and lacked sufficient sand to build up with rising sea level. Cape Elizabeth and the Crescent Beach areas were cut off from Saco River sand by Richmond Island, which acted as a barrier to longshore drift. Nevertheless, sand from the Saco River as well as from eroding bluffs near Bluff Island provided enough material for a nearly continuous barrier beach from Biddeford Pool to Richmond Island.

Sea level began to slow its rise by about 3,000 years ago, and the beaches and marshes of Saco Bay began to accumulate substantial deposits of sand and mud as a result. Sea level was only about 10 feet lower than it is today, so most of the present-day features of the bay were in existence (fig. 2.16). Because of the slow rate of sea level rise, Old Orchard Beach grew seaward (accreted) during this period, and large dunes formed from the wind-

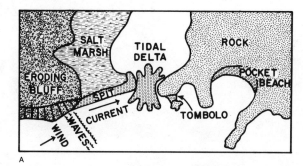

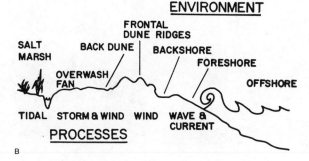

Figure 2.13. Major coastal environments along the Maine coast: (a) plan view of coast showing typical sorts of beaches and processes; (b) cross section of typical beach indicating zones and processes.

A

B

Figure 2.14. (a) Storm overwash fans on Jasper Beach, Maine; (b) as material moves landward during storms, the slow rise in sea level exposes trees and salt marsh peat in the beach face.

blown sand were left behind as the beach widened seaward. These "paleodunes" may be seen in the Ferry Beach or Scarborough Beach State Park areas today. After the beach connecting Bluff Island to Prouts Neck was broken, no more sand from the Saco River reached the Scarborough Beach area. Nevertheless, large old dunes remain covered by pine forests in that area today, dating from this earlier period. Massacre Pond, at the entrance to Scarborough Beach State Park, was probably a tidally connected bay at this time (fig. 2.16).

Although the Old Orchard Beach shoreline has remained in nearly the same place for the past 3,000 years, several important changes have occurred within historic times. Dams were erected on the Saco River during the colonial period and have probably trapped a large quantity of sand that would have become beach material. At the mouth of the Saco River the U.S. Army Corps of Engineers built rock jetties in the late nineteenth century to promote safe navigation (fig. 2.17). When they removed an enormous sand bar at the mouth of the river, this material was added to the land at Camp Ellis and built upon. The new land was not maintained by sand from the river, however, and soon disappeared. It is suspected by most geologists that the sand traveled north along the beach and led to the growth of Pine Point (fig. 2.17). This growth probably contributed to the closing of an unnamed inlet at the Old Orchard–Scarborough town lines and led to the closing of the Scarborough River inlet. Navigation problems here prompted the Corps of Engineers to construct a jetty on this inlet in the 1960s to hold back sand and maintain a channel. Dredged, sandy spoils from this

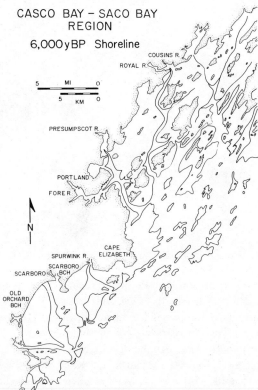

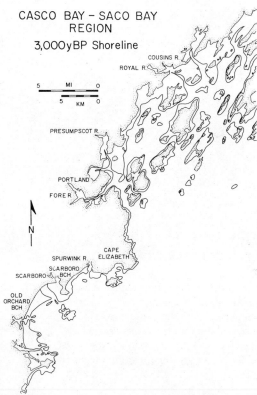

Figure 2.15. The coast of Casco and Saco bays approximately 6,000 years ago when sea level was about 60 feet lower than today. The stippled area represents the present-day shoreline.

Figure 2.16. The coast of Casco and Saco bays approximately 3,000 years ago when sea level was about 10 feet lower than today. The stippled area represents the present-day shoreline.

A

B

Figure 2.17. The two major river mouths of Saco Bay: (a) at Camp Ellis the Army Corps of Engineers built coastal engineering structures that later came to threaten the houses; (b) Pine Point formed during the late nineteenth and into the twentieth centuries as sand moved in from Camp Ellis and the beach to the southwest. The jetty at the mouth of the Scarborough River was built to keep sand out of the inlet channel.

channel were dumped on Pine Point and recently built upon.

In conjunction with growth of the Old Orchard Beach system, the Scarborough Marsh has also evolved. Borings in the marsh reveal that about 3,000 years ago the present marsh was probably an extensive sand flat. As the beach grew in front of it and offered protection from waves, salt marsh plants flourished and began to trap mud. This was the most extensive and productive marsh in Maine until human modification began to degrade it in the late nineteenth century. First a road was built to Pine Point that transformed the back-barrier portion of the marsh into a freshwater wetland. Then the railroad crossed the marsh and resulted in considerable filling along its length. Later, Route 1 was built across the upper marsh, and, finally, a sewer line was constructed across the marsh in the 1970s. Filling for construction of houses and businesses has occurred all around the marsh's margins, and its streams are no longer free to meander due to the network of roads, rails, and sewer lines crossing it. The most recent threat to the marsh is a proposal by the Corps of Engineers to dredge an anchorage in the tidal delta of the inlet. The removal of a large volume of sediment may have a deleterious impact on local wildlife and adversely reduce the sediment supply to the marsh.

The Saco Bay beach and marsh systems have changed from vigorous and growing environments several hundred years ago to sediment-starved, engineered regions adjacent to massive and growing human developments. If the scenario of rapidly rising future sea levels predicted by the U.S. Environmental Protection Agency holds true, this area will once again shift to a landward-migrating beach and sand flat system to the detriment of those who built in the area to enjoy it.

Casco Bay—large muddy estuaries

Mud flats surrounded by forested bluffs are often placid and do not seem as dynamic a coastal environment as sand beaches. Using Casco Bay as an example, however, we will consider the geological activities that have shaped the extensive mud flat shoreline of Maine.

About 9,000 years ago the shoreline of Casco Bay was also 200 feet beneath present sea level and existed 10 miles offshore of Portland (fig. 2.12). The large rivers that had carved the embayment of Casco Bay in preglacial times no longer entered the bay because their deep channels were blocked with glacial and postglacial marine sediment. Thus the Androscoggin and Kennebec rivers veer away from their 200-foot deep former channels in Freeport and Brunswick and join to enter the sea together in Merrymeeting Bay. All the streams presently entering Casco Bay originate in the coastal lowland formed during the marine drowning 12,500 years ago. As a result, the rivers of Casco Bay, the Presumpscot, Royal, Fore, and Cousins, are all small, slow-moving, muddy streams, which have only recently become etched in the former seafloor muds of the Presumpscot formation.

The northeast-southwest orientation of erosion-resistant ridges of bedrock constrained the early rivers of Casco Bay to flow in those directions for much of their length. Where the combined rivers entered the sea they probably dumped enormous quantities of mud onto the deepening Gulf of Maine. Most of this mud probably originated from landslides on the unstable slopes of the now-exposed former seafloor. A landslide deposit with preserved spruce trees estimated to be 11,000 years old has recently been described from the Bramhall Hill area of Portland.

As sea level rose across Casco Bay 6,000 years ago, the coastline began to change far more rapidly than that of nearby Saco Bay (fig. 2.15). The soft bluffs of marine mud yielded to the rising sea level in a continuous series of slumps that left higher ridges of bedrock barren of sediment as sea level drowned them. The river valleys became long, narrow estuaries with mud flats much like the present Damariscotta and Sheepscot estuaries. Salt marshes also may have existed on the landward fringes of the landslide deposits, but intertidal environments were generally smaller at this time because the tidal range was probably less.

By 3,000 years ago Casco Bay had begun to take on its present shape (fig. 2.16). The outer bay, seaward of the Cliff-Peaks-Long-Chebeague Island chain, had lost most of its former glacial and estuarine sediment to erosion by waves as the shoreline passed across the area. As a result, today it is rocky except in the old river channels where mud slumps still occasionally occur. The prominent islands of Casco Bay offered protection from waves to the inner area. Here, bluffs of glacial mud slowly eroded back, slump by slump, and left a well-preserved record of geological events on the bay bottom.

The past 3,000 years have been a time of slow drowning and bluff erosion. It has been suggested that the course of the Presumpscot and Fore rivers have even been changed by prehistoric landslides. The landslides of Casco Bay have been important to the development of the bay and essential to its biological productivity (figs. 2.18, 2.19). The erosion of coastal bluffs has been a major source of mud for the region's productive flats and possibly its deeper offshore waters. Bluff erosion can also be a local source for beach sand, a source that is blocked when seawalls and revetments are built to slow bluff retreat.

A major disturbance occurred in Casco Bay 200 years ago when European colonists arrived and deforested the coastal region for timber and agriculture. Coastal erosion probably accelerated at this time due to the loss of vegetation on bluffs. Much of the eroded sediment formed salt marshes and led to shoaling and closing of harbors like Mast, Porters, and Bungunac landings. As soon as dams were built on the bay's rivers and secondary growth was established on bluffs, however, the supply of mud was turned off and the marshes and bluffs again began to retreat. This retreat continues to the present, and most bluffs with houses on top have seawalls to slow down erosion.

In those few areas where sandy glacial deposits are eroding, beaches may occasionally form. These temporary pocket beaches lie between rocky points and only last as long as their eroding source (fig. 2.20). Many of the shoals or shallow intertidal areas between Casco Bay's many islands are beaches that drowned when their supply of sand was washed away.

As sea level continues to rise, the process that formed the Casco Bay shoreline will continue to operate. Most conspicuously, erosion of the bluffs of glacio-marine sediment will increasingly threaten property owners who built too close to the bluff edges. Construction of seawalls along the bluffs will slow this down, but it will also cut off the supply of new mud to marshes and flats. The marshes will probably continue to retreat, and flats will become reduced in area and productivity due to a lack of sediment. Dredging for new marinas in shallow, muddy areas will further reduce the amount of mud available to coastal systems and may lead to their degradation. The few beaches in the bay will disappear unless

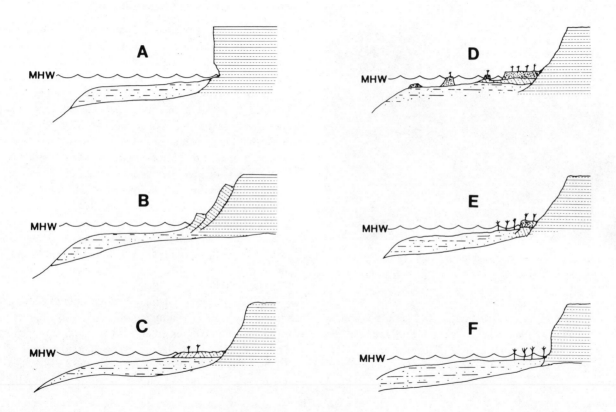

Figure 2.18. Bluff erosion and salt marsh formation in coastal Maine.

Figure 2.19. Salt marshes developed on slump blocks of Ice Age mud in Casco Bay. The marshes themselves are eroding, and, when gone, renewed slumping will occur.

new sand is eroded from bluffs or trucked in. The latter possibility has been considered for Willard Beach, in South Portland. The price of sand is high, however, and in light of its anticipated brief residence on the beach, nourishment is prohibitively expensive for the time being.

Beaches: the dynamic equilibrium

An understanding of coastal change can be summarized by the concept that shorelines are the result of a balance between the materials making up the coast and the processes operating on those materials. We will look at the beach as an example.

The beach is one of the earth's most dynamic environments. The beach—or zone of active sand movement—is always changing and always migrating, and we now know that it does so in accordance with the earth's natural laws. The natural laws of the beach control a beautiful, logical environment that builds up when the weather is good, and strategically (but only temporarily) retreats when confronted by big storm waves. This system depends on four factors: waves, sea level rise, beach sand, and shape of the beach. The relationship among these factors is a natural balance referred to as *dynamic equilibrium*: when one factor changes, the others adjust accordingly to maintain a balance. When we enter the system incorrectly—as we often do—the dynamic equilibrium continues to function but in a way that is harmful.

Answers to the following questions about beaches may clarify the nature of this dynamic equilibrium. It is important to keep in mind that the beach is an area where sand is moved by waves. Thus it extends from the toe of the dune to a depth of 30 to 40 feet offshore. The deeper beach region is the zone of sand movement during storms. The part on which we walk is only the upper beach.

How does the beach respond to a storm?

Old-timers and storm survivors have frequently commented on how flat and broad the beach is after a storm. The flat beach can be explained in terms of the dynamic equilibrium. As wave energy increases, the dunes at the back of the beach are eroded and sand is moved across the beach, changing its shape. The reason for this storm response is logical. The beach flattens itself so that storm waves expend their energy over a broader and more level surface. On a steeper surface storm-wave energy would be expended on a smaller area, causing greater damage. In summary, the waves take sand from the upper beach or the first dune and transport it to the lower beach. If a hot dog stand or beach cottage happens to be located on the first dune, it may disappear along with the dune sands.

A shore can lose a great deal of sand during a storm. Much of it will come back, however, gradually pushed shoreward by fair weather waves. As the sand returns to the beach, the wind takes over and slowly rebuilds the dunes, storing sand to respond to nature's next storm call. In order for the sand to come back, of course, there should be no man-made obstructions—such as a seawall—between the first dune and the beach. Return of the beach may take months or even years.

Sometimes besides simply flattening, a storm beach also will develop one or more offshore bars. The bars serve the function of tripping the large waves long before they reach the beach. The sand bar produced by storms is easily visible during calm weather as a line of surf a few to tens of yards off the beach. Geologists refer to the bar as a ridge and the intervening trough as a runnel.

How does the beach widen?

Beaches grow seaward in several ways, principally by (1) bringing in new sand by the so-called *longshore* (surf zone) *currents,* or (2) bringing in new sand from offshore by forming a *ridge and runnel* system. Actually these two ways of beach widening are not mutually exclusive.

Longshore currents are familiar to anyone who has swum in the ocean; they are the reason you sometimes end up somewhere down the beach, away from your towel. We commonly refer to this as the "undertow." Such currents result from waves approaching the beach at an angle, which causes a portion of the energy of the breaking wave to be directed along the beach. When combined with breaking waves, the weak current is capable of carrying large amounts of very coarse material for miles along the beach. The sand transported along the shore may be deposited at the end of a headland as a spit or tombolo (fig. 2.13).

Sand bars formed during small summer storms virtually march onto the shore and are "welded" to the beach. The next time you are at the beach, observe the offshore ridge for a period of a few days and verify this for yourself. You may find that each day you have to swim out a slightly shorter distance to stand on the sand bar.

At low tide during the summer the beach frequently has a trough filled or partly filled with water. This trough is formed by the ridge that is in the final stages of welding onto the beach. Several ridges combine to make the berm, or beach terrace, on which sunbathers loll.

Where does beach sand come from?

Sand may be carried onshore from the adjacent continental shelf, pushed up to the beach by fair-weather waves. Additional sand is brought in laterally by longshore currents that move in the surf zone parallel to the beach. Erosion of bluffs may contribute sand directly to beaches, and some sediment may be contributed locally at the heads of embayments by rivers and streams.

It is important for beach dwellers to know about or at least have some sense of the source of sand for their beach. If, for example, there is a lot of transported longshore sand in front of your favorite beach, the beach may well disappear if someone builds a groin "upstream." Community actions taken on an adjacent beach or inlet potentially could affect your beach, just as your action may affect your coastal neighbors.

Why do beaches erode?

As we have already pointed out, *beach erosion* is the cottage owner's term for the larger process called *shoreline migration*. Its principal cause is the sea level rise—presently judged to average about 1 foot per century along American shores. But averages can be misleading, and a 3-feet-per-century rise is typical along the New England coast. (Sea level rise can be different in different coastal areas because the land also may be slowly sinking or rising relative to sea level.)

Working in conjunction with the rise in sea level are the many forces of nature at the shore, including waves, tides, and the wind. These forces are aided and abetted by the effects that we create: jetties, groins, dams on rivers, and perhaps even the tracks cut into the sand by beach vehicles.

If most ocean shorelines are eroding, what is the long-range future of beach development?

The long-range future of beach development will depend on how individual communities respond to their migrating shoreline. Those communities that choose to protect their front-side houses at all costs need only look to portions of the New Jersey shore to see the end result. The life span of houses can unquestionably be extended by "stabilizing" a beach (slowing the erosion). The ultimate cost of slowing erosion, however, is loss of the beach. The length of time required for destruction of the beach is highly variable and depends on the shoreline or beach dynamics. Usually an extensive

Figure 2.20. Erosion of small bluffs provided sand for Willard Beach and other pocket beaches like it. The low bluffs are presently covered with residences and protected by seawalls. Because of the cutoff of "new" sand from bluffs, the beach is slowly eroding.

seawall on a barrier beach will do the trick in 10 to 30 years. Often a single storm will permanently remove a beach in front of a seawall.

If, when the time comes, a community grits its teeth and moves the front row of buildings or lets it fall in, the beaches can be saved in the long run. Unfortunately, so far in America, the primary factor involved in shoreline decisions, which every beach community must sooner or later make, has been money. Poor communities let the island roll on. Rich ones attempt to stop it.

The future of shoreline development in the United States appears to be one of increasing the expenditure of money which leads to the increasing loss of beach.

What can I do about my eroding beach?

This question has no simple answer but it is briefly addressed in chapter 3. If you are talking about an open-ocean shoreline, there is nothing you can do unless (1) you are wealthy or (2) the Corps of Engineers steps in. Your best response, especially from an environmental standpoint, is to move your threatened cottage elsewhere. The bottom line in trying to stop erosion of an open-ocean shoreline is that the methods employed will ultimately increase the erosion rate. For example, the simple act of hiring a friendly bulldozer operator to push sand up from the lower beach will steepen its profile and cause the beach to erode more rapidly during the next storm. Pumping in new sand (replenishment) costs a great

deal of money, and in most cases the artificial beach will disappear much more rapidly than its natural predecessor.

There are many ways to stop erosion in the short run if lots of money is available, but in the long run erosion cannot be halted except at the cost of losing the natural beach. Chapter 3 examines the options of shoreline engineering.

3 Man and the shoreline

Shoreline engineering: stabilizing the unstable

The coastline of Maine is much more diverse and has experienced more rapid geological change than most other coastal states. Within a stretch of 10 miles one may see rocky cliffs, long sand beaches, salt marshes, mud flats, or "cobble" beaches complexly juxtaposed in an environmental collage. As discussed in the last chapter, the key to understanding coastal environmental diversity is generally simple: bedrock controls the overall coastal geometry (that is, the location of points and bays); eroding glacial deposits determine the nature of intertidal sediment (that is, mud flats or sand beaches); and modern physical processes (that is, waves, wind, currents) regulate the movement of material from one place to another. Generally, sand and mud are delivered to the shoreline by eroding glacial deposits or rivers. Wind blows sand into dunes, and waves move sand along spits. Tidal currents carry muddy water through inlets and redistribute material on marshes and flats. The "silent partner" to all this is the slow, inexorable rise of the ocean, which moves all environments landward and upward toward higher ground.

Shoreline engineering is a general phrase that refers to any method of changing or altering the natural shoreline system in order to stabilize it. Methods of stabilizing shorelines range from simply planting dune grass to constructing massive seawalls using draglines, cranes, and bulldozers. The benefits of such methods are usually short-lived. Locally, shoreline engineering may actually cause shoreline retreat as evidenced by the beach in Camp Ellis adjacent to the Corps of Engineers' jetty (figs. 3.1, 2.17a). Beach erosion caused by man may be greater than that of natural processes.

The coastline of Maine has fewer engineering mistakes on it than most other states (New Jersey and Florida, for example), but this is because relatively few large projects have been carried out on its sandy beaches. Where such projects have occurred, Maine's coast has suffered. In the 1960s, for example, the U.S. Army Corps of Engineers agreed to construct a harbor for the town of Wells, Maine, on the location of a tidal delta near an inlet. At a cost of more than $.5 million the inlet was "stabilized" with long rock jetties on either side and a channel dredged from the inlet opening to the former tidal delta (fig. 3.2). The sandy spoils from the project were unceremoniously dumped on the adjacent salt marsh. Twenty years have passed and the harbor has long since filled again, but further dredging has been prevented by the town. It appears that the jetties have trapped sand that formerly was exchanged between the beach and the tidal inlet and delta. Now the beach is mostly eroding and homeowners there want no more dredging. The harbor remains practically useless, while developers are now eyeing the dredge spoils as a site to construct new vacation homes. Clearly, the economic and environmental price of stabilizing coastal regions is great, and

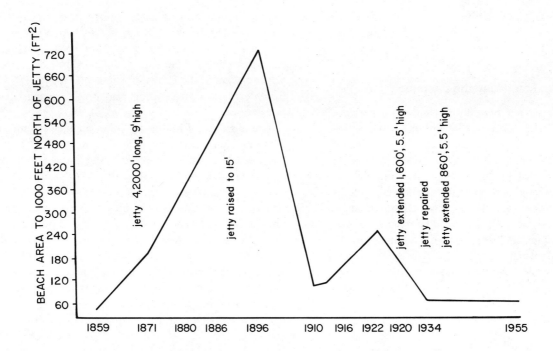

Figure 3.1. Changes in the beach area at Camp Ellis between the 1850s and 1950s. Growth of the beach was caused by removal of a delta at the river mouth, and erosion was related to jetty construction. (Modified from Ferland, 1979.)

Figure 3.2. Wells Harbor in 1970. Note the large pile of sandy spoils dumped in the salt marsh and the accumulation of sand at the side of the jetty. In a state known for its deep natural harbors, the siting of Wells "Harbor" on a tidal delta is folly. Maine Geological Survey file photo.

public awareness of the magnitude of the problem is essential. There are, of course, situations in which stabilization and dredging are essential. Channels leading to major ports like Portland and Bath must always be maintained.

There are three major ways by which shorelines are stabilized.

These methods are listed below, in decreasing order of environmental safety.

Beach replenishment

If you must repair a beach, this is probably the gentlest approach. Replenishment consists of bringing new sand to a beach and reconstructing the former dunes and upper beach. No project ever has enough money to replenish an entire beach out to a depth of 30 or 40 feet where waves begin to move the sand. Thus only the upper beach is covered with new sand, making the beach steeper than before. The new, artificially steepened beach profile is often unstable, however, and rapid loss of sand frequently occurs. For example, sand has often been placed in front of the eroding houses of Camp Ellis. Too little sand and too much seawall have always led to its rapid disappearance.

At present Maine's laws require that new beach sand be approximately the same size as the material it replaces. In practice this is difficult to achieve because replenishment sand for Maine's beaches usually comes from a nearby inlet channel, bay bottom, or borrow pit on the mainland. Frequently this material consists of grains larger than the natural beach sand and may behave differently. For example, the Soil Conservation Service constructed new sand dunes on Ogunquit Beach in 1974 to repair damage caused by a blizzard and protect a sewage treatment plant on that beach (fig. 3.3). Unfortunately, the new dune sand was dredged from the nearby Ogunquit River channel and contained coarse sand

Figure 3.3. The Ogunquit dune is a pile of coarse sand and gravel thinly covered by dune plants. Storm damage here will not be easily repaired by natural processes. Note the sewage treatment plant at the center. Photo taken at low tide.

and gravel instead of fine, windblown sand. This new "dune," although vegetated with beach grass, will never behave like a real dune because the wind cannot blow the sand back into place if it is moved by storm waves. Although better than no dunes at all, more thoughtful selection of replenishment sand here would have gone a long way toward providing a more aesthetically pleasing and functional sand dune system.

Although beneficial for a time, the cost of beach replenishment may be prohibitively expensive in the long run. The Corps of Engineers estimates that Willard Beach in South Portland (fig. 2.20) will initially require $500,000 of sandy replenishment fill, to be followed by periodic costly nourishment. The Corps calls such projects "ongoing," but "eternal" is a more honest term.

One sort of beach replenishment seems almost peculiar to Maine, unfortunately. Because we have so few sand beaches, particularly in the area north of Cape Elizabeth, some individuals and towns have dumped sand on mud flats to make beaches. There are several problems with this practice. Since the sand was not brought to the beach by natural forces, it is also not maintained by them and erodes quickly. When the sand leaves the "beach" it usually ends up where no one wants it, like in a navigation channel or on a mud flat. In Brunswick the continued replenishment of sand for the artificial Thomas Point Beach has led to the degradation of valuable mud flats containing state seed clams and bloodworms (fig. 3.4).

Figure 3.4. Thomas Point Beach is an artificial beach near Brunswick. An eroding bluff has been covered with sand to the misfortune of the seed clam flat that exists seaward of the "beach." The practice of nourishing this beach has been discontinued by a State Board of Environmental Protection decision.

Despite the difficulties involved with replenishment, it is less harmful to the dynamic equilibrium of beaches than the following methods.

Groins and jetties

Groins and jetties are walls built perpendicular to the shoreline. Groins are relatively small features (hundreds of feet long) built on straight stretches of beach away from inlets. They are intended to trap sand flowing in the longshore (surf zone) current. When a groin is working, more sand should be trapped on one side than the other. The problem with groins is that while one side of the structure gains sand, the other side loses it. As a result, more groins are built on the eroding, downdrift side, and eventually the beach becomes a veritable obstacle course of groins. Such structures litter once-beautiful beaches like Miami Beach and Cape May, New Jersey. The short-term gain of groins is more than offset by their great cost, long-term damage, and generally ugly appearance. They are illegal at the present time in Maine, and none exist here.

Jetties are similar to groins, but much larger (sometimes a mile or more). They are usually built adjacent to inlets or rivers to prevent sand from filling the channel. In Maine jetties built by the Army Corps of Engineers exist adjacent to the mouths of the Kennebunk, Webhannet (Wells), Saco, and Scarborough rivers. In the case of the Webhannet and Scarborough rivers much sand has accumulated on the beach side of the jetties. Unfortunately, in the case of Wells, this sand has come from Wells Beach, never to return—it is now covered with residences (fig. 3.2). The accumulation of sand on one side of the Scarborough River jetty has led to property damage on Pine Point on the other side (fig. 2.17). Curiously, the long jetty at Camp Ellis has trapped sand in the Saco River and led to channel shoaling. This in turn has deprived adjacent Camp Ellis of sand and led to severe erosion there. For these reasons jetties are presently outlawed in Maine.

Other structures

Seawalls, bulkheads, and revetments are members of a family
of coastal engineering structures built back from and parallel to
the shoreline. Constructed of wood or stone, they are designed to
withstand wave impact during daily high tides (seawalls) or during
storms (bulkheads). The construction of one of these features is a
very drastic measure on a beach and harms the surrounding area in
the following ways:

1. It reflects wave energy, ultimately removing the beach and
steepening the offshore profile. This damage occurs over a period
of one to 30 years. The steepened offshore profile increases the
storm wave energy striking the shoreline, which in turn increases
erosion.

2. It increases the intensity of longshore currents, hastening
removal of the beach (figs. 3.5 and 3.6).

3. It prevents the exchange of sand between dunes and beach.
Thus the beach cannot supply new sand to the dunes or flatten as
it tends to do during storms.

4. It concentrates wave and current energy at the ends of the
wall, increasing erosion at these points.

Building a seawall is an irreversible act with limited benefits. A
seawall gradually removes the beach in front of it and must eventually be replaced with a bigger, "better," more expensive wall.
While a seawall may extend the lives of coastal structures in normal weather, it cannot protect structures on low-lying barrier spits
from the havoc of major northeasters, and it cannot stop overwash
or storm surges. The Surf Street seawall, for example, has required far more money for repairs following storms than the value
of the road it protects (fig. 3.6). For these reasons seawalls are
presently banned from Maine except in "unique" circumstances.
Where seawalls already exist, such as Camp Ellis and Wells, they
may be maintained but cannot be enlarged. According to current
regulations, if a seawall and adjacent property are destroyed by a
storm, they must be removed.

Retaining walls are similar in design to seawalls, but their purpose is to hold back eroding bluffs. The walls may be made of
concrete, wood, or stone, but local boulders in wire mesh are
a very popular design. Like seawalls, retaining walls are ineffective
over the long run and often prove to be their own worst enemy
(fig. 3.7). By reflecting wave energy they prevent marshes from
colonizing the toe of an eroding bluff and lead to undermining
(fig. 2.18). While the wall may protect an exposed bluff from
waves, groundwater still seeps through the earth and leads to large
slumps. So long as retaining walls are effective, essential sand and
mud is prevented from leaving the bluff and building beaches and
mud flats. Retaining walls in existence on Great Hill in Kennebunk
and planned for the Rogue Bluffs area may eventually lead to the
loss of local beaches if they are not first destroyed by nature.

The long-range effect of seawalls can be seen in New Jersey
and Miami Beach. In Monmouth Beach, New Jersey, the town
building inspector recounted the town's seawall history. Pointing
to a seawall, he said, "There were once houses and even farms
in front of that wall. First we built small seawalls, and they were

1. BEFORE THE WALL

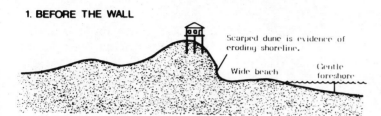

Scarped dune is evidence of eroding shoreline.

Wide beach

Gentle foreshore

2. WALL CONSTRUCTED

Development proceeds as buyers believe property is protected by the wall.

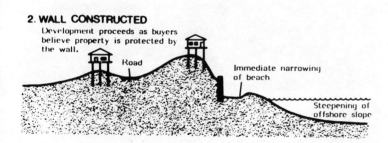

Road

Immediate narrowing of beach

Steepening of offshore slope

3. TWO TO FORTY YEARS LATER

There is no beach. The wall is overwashed by storms, and wave energy is now undermining and steepening the offshore slope.

4. TEN TO SIXTY YEARS LATER   (New Jerseyization)

Bigger, "better" reinforced seawall is put in.

As depth increases, wave size increases; therefore a higher wall is needed.

ULTIMATE RESULTS: Development is behind wall, no beach is available, and the sea floor is cluttered with fallen walls and groins.

Figure 3.5. Saga of a seawall.

Figure 3.6. The seawall protecting Surf Street, Saco, as seen at low tide. Despite its great cost and damage to the adjacent "beach," this structure repeatedly collapses during winter storms.

Figure 3.7. Construction of a retaining wall in Addison, Maine, may protect property for a while, but the supply of mud is cut off to nearby salt marshes.

destroyed by the storms that seemed to get bigger and bigger. Now we have come to this huge wall which we hope will hold." The wall he spoke of, adjacent to the highway, was high enough to prevent even a glimpse of the sea beyond. There was no beach in front of it, but remnants of old seawalls, groins, and bulkheads extended hundreds of yards into the sea.

A philosophy of shoreline conservation: "We have met the enemy and he is us"

In 1801 Postmaster Ellis Hughes of Cape May, New Jersey, placed the following advertisement in the *Philadelphia Aurora*:

The subscriber has prepared himself for entertaining company who uses sea bathing and he is accommodated with extensive house room with fish, oysters, crabs, and good liquors. Care will be taken of gentlemen's horses. Carriages may be driven along the margin of the ocean for miles and the wheels will scarcely make an impression upon the sand. The slope of the shore is so regular that persons may wade a great distance. It is the most delightful spot that citizens can go in the hot season.

This was the first beach advertisement in America and sparked the beginning of the American rush to the shore.

In the next 75 years six U.S. presidents vacationed at Cape May. At the time of the Civil War it was certainly the country's most prestigious beach resort. The resort's prestige continued into the twentieth century. In 1908 Henry Ford raced his newest-model cars on Cape May beaches.

Today Cape May no longer appears on anyone's list of great beach resorts. The problem is not that the resort is too old-fashioned, but that no beach remains (fig. 3.8).

Cape May city officials in recent years applied for a federal grant to build groins to "save the beaches." Though it is possible that these officials exaggerated their problems in order to increase their chances of receiving funds, the point of their application was clear:

Our community is nearly financially insolvent. The economic consequences of beach erosion are depriving all our people of much needed municipal services. . . . The residents of

Figure 3.8. Cape May, New Jersey, seawall (1976).

one area of town, Frog Hollow, live in constant fear. The Frog Hollow area is a 12 block segment of the town which becomes submerged when the tide is merely 1 to 2 feet above normal. The principal reason is that there is no beach fronting on this area. . . . Maps show blocks that have been lost, a boardwalk that has been lost. . . . The stone wall, one mile long, which we erected along the ocean front only five years ago has already begun to crumble from the pounding of the waves since there is little or no beach. . . . We have finally reached a point where we no longer have beaches to erode.

Maine will not have to wait a century and a half for this crisis to reach its shores. The pressure to develop is here and increasing. Many of our beaches, like Moody Beach, Kinney Shores, Drakes Island, and others, have long rows of houses with no sand dunes seaward of them. They have seawalls which will never offer protection from large storms, but which will increasingly lead to beach loss or narrowing. Old Orchard is already seeing the permanent high-rise monoliths of New Jerseyization crowding and shading its shores. Old Orchard Beach is generally fronted by seawalls, and this once grand beach is inexorably narrowing. In the words of an early geological researcher of Old Orchard: "The central section of Old Orchard Beach has changed in historic time from a beach with a 600-foot wide, flat, low tide terrace with a firm surface allowing horses, carriages, and automobile races to occur in an area where a steep, soft, coarse beach with a 100- to 200-foot wide low tide terrace exists today. This change over 80 years seems

definitely to be related to the stoppage of continuous sand-sized sediment supply" (S. Farrell, 1972, p. 124).

Like the original Cape May resort, our structures are not placed far back from the shore, nor have we prudently placed structures behind dunes or on high ground. Consequently, Maine's coastal development is no less vulnerable to the rising sea than was Cape May's, and no shoreline engineering device will prevent its ultimate destruction. The solution lies in recognizing certain truths about the shoreline.

Truths of the shoreline

Cape May is the country's oldest shoreline resort. Built on a shoreline that migrates somewhat like Maine's (but more slowly), it is a classic example of the poorly developed American shoreline, and one from which Mainers can learn.

From the experiences of Cape May and other shoreline areas, certain generalizations about the shoreline emerge quite clearly. These truths are equally evident to scientists who have studied the shoreline and to old-timers who have lived there all their lives. As aids to safe and aesthetically pleasing shoreline development, these truths should be the fundamental basis of planning.

Erosion is not a problem until a structure is built on a shoreline. Beach or bluff erosion is a common, expected event, not a natural disaster. Shoreline erosion in its natural state is not a threat to coasts. When a beach retreats, the coast is not disappearing;

it is only migrating. When a bluff slumps, the vitality of the marshes and flats is enhanced, not diminished. Many developed shorelines are migrating at surprisingly rapid rates, though only the few investigators who pore over historic aerial photographs are aware of it. Whether the beach is growing or shrinking does not concern the visiting swimmer, surfer, hiker, or fisherman. It is when man builds a "permanent" structure in this zone of change that a problem develops.

Construction by man on the shoreline causes shoreline changes. The sandy beach is a delicate balance of sand supply, beach shape, wave energy, and sea level rise. Most construction on or near the shoreline changes this balance and reduces the natural flexibility of the beach. The resulting changes often threaten man-made structures. Dune removal, which often precedes construction, reduces the sand supply used by the beach to adjust its profile during storms. Beach cottages—even those on stilts—may obstruct the normal sand exchange between the beach and the shelf during storms. Similarly, engineering devices interrupt or modify the natural cycle. Bulkheads built to protect portions of bluffs often hasten erosion of adjacent areas.

Shoreline engineering protects the interests of a very few, often at a very high cost in federal and state dollars. Shoreline engineering is carried out to save coastal property, not the coast itself. Beach stabilization projects are in the interest of the minority of beach property owners rather than the public. If the shoreline were allowed to migrate naturally over and past the cottages and hot dog stands, the fisherman and swimmer would not suffer. Yet beach property owners apply pressure for the spending of public funds to protect the beach. Since these property owners do not constitute the general public, their personal interests may not warrant the large expenditures of public money required for shoreline stabilization.

Exceptions to this rule are the beaches near large metropolitan areas. The combination of extensive high-rise development and heavy beach use may afford ample economic justification for extensive and continuous shoreline stabilization projects. The cost of replenishing a half mile of Moody-Wells Beach is about equal to the cost of replenishing one-half mile of Coney Island Beach near New York City, which accommodates tens of thousands more people daily during the summer months. It is more justifiable to spend tax money to replenish the latter beach, since protection of this beach is clearly in the interest of the public that pays for it.

Shoreline engineering destroys the beach it was intended to save. Incredible as it sounds, New Jersey has miles of "well-protected" shoreline—without beaches! Figure 3.9 shows the "beach" that costs Virginia Beach, Virginia, $20 million a year to maintain.

The cost of saving beach property through shoreline engineering is usually greater than the value of the property to be saved. Price estimates of the costs of shoreline engineering are often unrealistically low in the long run for a variety of reasons. The cost of maintenance, repairs, and replacement is typically underestimated because it is erroneously assumed that the big storm, capable of removing an entire beach replenishment project overnight, will somehow bypass the area. Moreover, planners often view the in-

Figure 3.9. Virginia Beachless.

evitable northeaster as a catastrophic act of God or a sudden stroke of bad luck for which no one can plan. Most cost evaluations also ignore the increased potential for damage resulting from shoreline engineering. In fact, very few shoreline engineering projects would be funded at all if those controlling the purse strings realized that such "lines of defense" must be perpetual.

Once shoreline engineering is begun, it cannot be stopped. Shoreline history throughout the world confirms this statement. Such engineering must be maintained indefinitely because of the long-range damage caused to the beach it "protects." By keeping the sandy shoreline from migrating naturally, it steepens the beach profile, reduces the sand supply, and therefore accelerates erosion. Thus once man has installed a shoreline structure, "better" —larger or more expensive—structures must follow, only to suffer the same fate as their predecessors (fig. 3.9).

History shows us there are two situations that may terminate this cycle of shoreline engineering. First, a civilization may decline or disappear and thus no longer build and repair its structures; the ancient Romans, for example, built mighty seawalls. Second, a large storm may destroy a shoreline stabilization system so thoroughly that people decide to give up. Americans, however, usually regard such a storm as an engineering challenge and respond with continued shoreline stabilization projects. As noted previously, rubble from two or more generations of seawalls remain off some New Jersey beaches. The repeated failures of the seawalls at Camp Ellis (fig. 3.10) have led members of that community to propose that the Corps of Engineers erect a bigger, better wall to protect their property.

Questions to ask if shoreline engineering is proposed

When a community is considering some form of shoreline engineering, it is almost invariably done in an atmosphere of crisis. Buildings and commercial interests are threatened; time is short, an expert is brought in, and a solution is proposed. Under such

Figure 3.10. Seawalls at Camp Ellis. Beaches cannot exist here anymore because of the engineering structures.

circumstances the right questions are sometimes not asked. The following is a list of questions you might bring up if you find yourself a member of such a community.

1. Will the proposed solution to shoreline erosion damage the recreational beach? in 10 years? in 20 years? in 30 years? in 50 years?

2. How much will maintenance of the solution cost in 10 years? in 20 years? in 30 years? in 50 years?

3. If the proposed solution is carried out, what is likely to happen in the next big tropical storm? mild hurricane? severe northeaster?

4. What was the erosion rate of the shoreline here during the last 10 years? 20 years? since 1940 (the year of the first coastal aerial photography in Maine)? since the mid-1800s (the time when the first accurate Maine shoreline maps were surveyed by the old U.S. Geodetic Survey)?

5. What will the proposed solution do to the beachfront? Will the solution for one portion of a beach create problems for another portion?

6. What will happen if an adjacent inlet migrates or closes up?

7. If the proposed erosion solution is carried out, how will it affect type and density of future beachfront development? Will additional controls on beachfront development be needed at the same time as the solution?

8. What will happen 20 years from now if the inlet nearby is dredged for navigation? If jetties are constructed or enlarged on an adjacent inlet? If seawalls and groins are built on nearby beaches?

9. How will the proposed solution affect the 50- to 100-year environmental and economic prognosis for erosion if predictions of an accelerating sea level rise are accurate?

10. If stabilization—for instance a seawall—is permitted here, will this open the door to seawalls elsewhere on the beach?

11. What are the alternatives to the proposed solution to shoreline erosion? Should the threatened buildings be allowed to fall in? Should they be moved? Should tax money be used to move them?

12. What are the long-range environmental and economic costs of the various alternatives from the standpoint of the local property owners? the beach community? the entire town? the citizens of Maine and the rest of the country?

The solutions

1. Design to live with the flexible coastal environment. Don't fight nature with a "line of defense."

2. Consider all man-made structures near the shoreline temporary.

3. Accept any engineering scheme for beach restoration or preservation as a last resort, and then only for metropolitan areas.

4. Base decisions affecting coastal development on the welfare of the public rather than the minority of shorefront property owners.

5. Let the lighthouse, beach cottage, motel, or hot dog stand fall when its time comes.

4 Selecting a site on the Maine coast

No low-lying area can be considered completely safe, especially one adjacent to an ocean notorious for its fierce and destructive storms. Given the right conditions, storm, wave, wind, flood, or ice can erode and overwhelm almost any location on the coast. Furthermore, human activity, particularly construction, almost always lessens the relative stability of the natural environment. Man-made structures are static (immobile), and when placed in a dynamic (mobile) system they disrupt the balance of that system. Interference with sand and mud supply or movement, disruption of vegetative cover, topographic or bathymetric alteration, and similar effects of man-made structures actually create conditions favorable to the damage or loss of those structures.

Some coastal areas are considerably safer to live and build in than others. Structures placed in the least dynamic zones (stable areas less subject to movement or change) are least likely to incur damage. Areas, rates, and intensities of natural physical processes should, therefore, be the basis for choosing a safe homesite. Consider, for example, an inland river and the floodplain (flat area) next to the river channel. Even casual observation reveals that the river floods. Observation over a long period of time shows that the frequency and size of the floods follow a pattern. The area

adjacent to the river is flooded every spring. The entire floodplain is flooded only every five to 10 years. Once or twice in a lifetime the flood is devastating, covering an area greater than the floodplain. Detailed stream studies confirm these observations. Thus we can determine the frequency and size of floods in a given area, though we cannot predict exactly when one flood will occur. We may describe an individual flood as a one-in-ten-years flood, or a one-in-fifty-years flood, based on the frequency of a given flood level. Site analysis maps included in this chapter are indexed in figure 4.1.

Studies of past coastal storms and associated floods in New England form the basis for predicting the height and intensity of future floods (fig. 4.2). The Flood Insurance Rate Maps (FIRMS) produced by the Federal Emergency Management Agency (FEMA) incorporate past flood and wave heights into a model that predicts how often, within a 100-year period, similar depths of inundation will probably reoccur. They are not without drawbacks, however, because they are not yet available for all locations in coastal Maine and do not account for the continuing landward retreat of the coast. Thus, in addition to storm flood levels, one must consider other natural indicators of site safety and stability.

Stability indicators: some clues for the wise

In coastal regions a number of environmental attributes indicate the natural history of a given area. By revealing how dynamic an area has been through time, these attributes aid prospective builders in

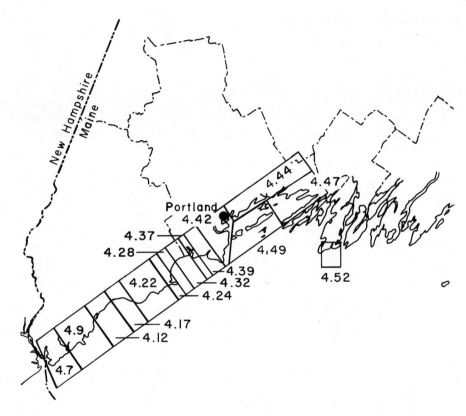

Figure 4.1. Index map delineating the boundaries of the following site analysis maps.

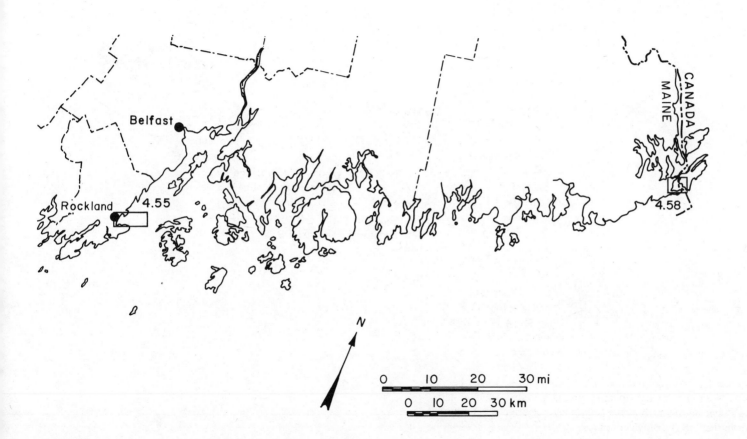

Belfast

Rockland   4.55

4.58

CANADA

MAINE

N

| 0 | 10 | 20 | 30 mi |

| 0 | 10 | 20 | 30 km |

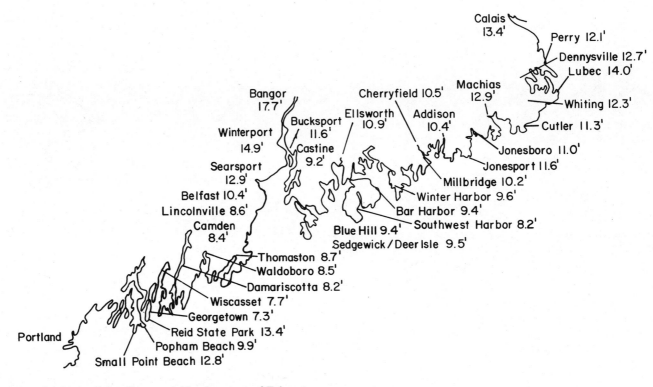

Figure 4.2. Depth of coastal flooding caused by the storm of February 2, 1976. Note that this damaging storm did not affect southwestern Maine's beaches as much as the central and eastern coast. (Information from the U.S. Geological Survey, 1979.)

deciding whether a site is safe for development. Natural indicators include vegetation, terrain, land elevation, and bedrock or soil type.

Vegetation

Vegetation may indicate environmental stability, age, and elevation. In general, the higher and thicker the plant growth, the more stable the site and the safer the area for development. Maritime forests grow only at elevations high enough to prevent frequent floods. Pitch pine forests in the landward areas of Popham Beach, Ferry Beach, Saco, or fronting Massacre Pond at Scarborough Beach take many years to form and cannot endure very frequent flooding by storms. Such heavily forested regions are usually (though not always) safe from coastal erosion and flooding. Similarly, gentle bluffs with old trees on their seaward slopes are usually stable and unlikely to slump. Steep bluffs, either unvegetated or partly covered with young grasses and shrubs, on the other hand, seriously indicate future erosion. In beach regions, unvegetated areas or locations covered only with American Beach Grass are sites that will likely be adversely affected by storms in the near future. Construction over marshes or mud flats (currently regulated by law; see chapter 5) for whatever purposes can be considered only temporary.

Terrain, elevation, bedrock

The factors of terrain, elevation, and the presence or absence of bedrock also measure an area's safety from various adverse natural processes. Low, flat areas are subject to wave attack and storm surge flooding. The flooding of barrier beaches may even occur from the landward marsh side. Figure 4.2 shows typical storm surge levels for many locations in coastal Maine. Construction over bedrock, all other factors being equal, is invariably safer than over a bluff composed of unconsolidated (loose) sand or mud. This is true because the rock is relatively unyielding to waves and floods, while the "soft" bluff will often collapse (fig. 4.3). Some sites are safe from floods due to their high elevation only until the moment they are undermined (fig. 4.3).

Coastal environments: boundaries of activity

Coastal areas may be divided into various zones or environments that indicate prevailing physical conditions (fig. 2.13). These environments include the beach, frontal dune, back dune fields, overwash fans, tidal inlets, maritime forests, salt and freshwater marshes and bogs, and upland bluffs. A builder and buyer should be able to identify and understand these environments to determine the safety of particular coastal areas for development.

A

B

Figure 4.3. Soft bluffs of sand and mud offer protection from floods until they are undermined: (a) Popham Beach, 1976; (b) Jonesport, 1985.

The beach

The sandy area seaward of the primary sand dunes or frontal dune ridges is the beach. This is certainly the most dangerous location for a house, regardless of its elevation. All the sand grains on a beach are put there by waves, and in the course of a typical year all are moved by waves. No seawall or groin system can protect beach property from the intensity of storms. No houses placed between Maine's sand dunes and the Atlantic Ocean will survive the next 100 years. For this reason, new construction on Maine's beaches is not permitted by law.

Frontal dunes

The dunes closest to the ocean are the primary, or frontal, dunes, although distinct ridges may be absent due to erosion. Such dunes serve as a sand reservoir that feeds the beach during storms (fig. 4.4). Their relatively great elevation provides a temporary line of defense against wind and waves both for the beach and any structures built landward of the dune line.

This line of defense is leaky, however, because of the overwash passes between the dunes. When man interferes with the dune system, both natural and man-made systems suffer. We must recognize the mobility of dune systems—even those stabilized by dune grasses. Dune buggies, foot traffic, drought, and fire destroy vegetation and therefore dune stability. By prohibiting vehicles on the dunes, and by building boardwalks and footbridges over them rather than building footpaths through them, we may preserve the dunes. Avoiding the construction of seawalls, groins, and bulkheads also preserves dunes by assuring that the sand flow feeding them is not interrupted.

If dunes are destroyed or threatened, some remedial steps can be taken to stabilize them artificially. Planting dune grass in bare areas stabilizes existing dunes and encourages additional dune growth. Snow fencing is commonly used to trap sand and to increase dune growth.

The high elevation of a dune does not in itself render a site safe. An area with a high erosion rate is likely to lose its dune protection during the average lifetime of a cottage (fig. 4.5). Even setback ordinances, which require that structures be placed a minimum distance behind the dune, do not guarantee long-term protection. Furthermore, if you locate on a primary dune, you can expect

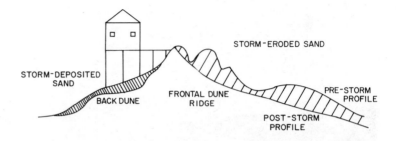

Figure 4.4. Topographic profiles across a beach before and after a storm. Eroded beach sand may travel offshore and move landward as washover deposit. A safely sited property is high above and landward of the flooded area. Contrast this with figure 3.5.

to lose your home, or experience damage during the next major storm.

Back dune fields

Dune fields are open, bare-to-grassy sand dune areas found between the primary dunes and the maritime forest, marsh, or bay landward of the shoreline. Some of these dunes are active, with the sand and dune positions continually shifting; other dune fields are stable and do not move much at all.

Stable dune fields offer sites that are relatively safe from wave erosion, overwash, and storm surge flooding—if the elevation is

Figure 4.5. Property loss in the back dune environment, Popham Beach, February 1984. The septic tank (foreground) and substrate for this house were removed in spite of the back dune setting and the absence of a major storm.

Figure 4.6. To comply with state regulations, new construction may occur only in the back dunes when the first living level is elevated 1 foot above the predicted 100-year flood elevation.

sufficiently high. However, digging up the dunes for construction may cause blowing sand, destabilize vegetation, and increase sand movement. At present construction is permitted in back dune areas that are relatively high (*A* or *C* flood zone) and unlikely to be eroded within the next 100 years. The first floor of permitted construction must be at least 1 foot above the predicted 100-year flood elevation, which usually means construction on posts (fig. 4.6).

Overwash fans and tidal inlets

The two major mechanisms for moving sand in a landward direction along a coast is through tidal inlets, and, during storms, across overwash fans. Owing to the large amount of development on many of Maine's large beaches, overwash fans are often common only near tidal inlets.

Tidal inlets are breaks in barrier spits where tidal waters enter to flood salt marshes (fig. 2.13). Their size and shape, where not dredged and stabilized by jetties, is controlled by the volume of water that must be exchanged by the tides. During a large storm much more water than "normal" enters an inlet, and still more water may exit on ebb tide if a river also exits through the inlet. Surplus water flattens dune fields near the inlet and leaves over-wash deposits on the landward side of the barrier. For this reason the region near an inlet is considered the least stable portion of a barrier beach system.

Inlets also have a tendency to migrate, rendering adjacent barrier areas more dangerous. In some locations where inlets are engi-neered, such as at Pine Point or Wells, there are places where the beach has accreted significantly adjacent to a jetty and overwash cannot occur (figs. 2.17B, 3.2). In these locations the margins of the channel are in danger of erosion due to channel migration or from waves generated by local boat traffic.

Along undeveloped beaches lacking an inlet or with a relatively small inlet, overwash is a more common phenomenon. Overwash fans are the sand and gravel deposits left by a storm on the land-ward side of a beach (fig. 2.14). Because of the danger to these sites during storms, current Maine law does not permit construc-tion on overwash fans.

Maritime forests

Woods, thickets, and shrub areas generally are the safest places for cottage construction. Under normal conditions overwash, flooding, and blowing sand are not problems in these environments. The plants stabilize the underlying sediment and offer a protective screen.

If you should build in a vegetated area, preserve as much vege-tation as possible, including undergrowth. Trees are excellent protection from flying debris during storms. Remove large dead trees from the construction site but conserve the surrounding forest to protect your home. Stabilize bare or cleared areas as soon as possible with new plantings.

Salt and freshwater marshes and bogs

Construction on salt marshes is prohibited in Maine because of their value as habitats for wildlife and buffers from floods (see chapter 5). Freshwater bogs, however, are not protected unless they are relatively large. These environments deserve protection for many of the same reasons marshes do. Furthermore, once fill and a building are placed on a bog surface, compaction can occur and lead to slow submergence of a site. Since many coastal freshwater bogs are separated from the sea only by a small barrier beach, these environments do not have a long-term safe future anyway.

Upland bluffs

The "soft coast" of Maine includes numerous bluffs of unconsoli-dated material. Often these bluffs are 5 to 35 feet high and appear to be quite safe from coastal storm or flood damage. The bluffs are composed of unconsolidated sand, gravel, or mud, however, and unlike bedrock cliffs they are prone to slumping and erosion. Building on a bluff slope is exceedingly dangerous because even a small slump could lead to substantial property loss. Preventing even small slumps can be very costly.

Site safety: rules for survival

To determine the safety of coastal sites it is necessary to evaluate all prevalent dynamic processes. Information on storm surge, overwash, erosion rate, inlet migration, longshore drift, and other processes may be obtained from maps, aerial photographs, scientific literature, or personal observations. Appendix C provides an annotated list of scientific sources; you are encouraged to obtain those of interest to you. Although developers and planners usually have the resources and expertise to use such information in making decisions, they sometimes ignore it. In the past the individual buyer was not likely to seek needed information in deciding on the suitability of a given site. Today's buyer should be better informed.

   To help the coastal dweller, we have drawn a series of diagrammatic maps that summarize information obtained from a cross section of scientific literature. Our conclusions, as represented on these maps, are based on published data, aerial photographs, and coastal maps, as well as our personal communications and observations. These maps divide the coastal region into "safe," "caution," and "danger" zones for development on the basis of the summarized information. Keep in mind, however, that small maps of large areas must be generalized and that every site must still be evaluated individually. Safe sites may exist in "danger" zones, while dangerous sites may exist in "safe" zones. Our understanding of the geology of coastal Maine is still naive, and, undoubtedly, more sophisticated maps will be produced in the future. Probably the best protection against purchasing unsafe coastal property is to employ a consulting geologist who has passed the state certification examination.

Summary checklist for site safety evaluation

The following is a list of properties that are essential to site safety (b = beach site; bl = bluff site):

— Site elevation is above anticipated storm surge level (b).
— Site is behind a natural protective barrier such as a line of sand dunes (b).
— Site is well away from a migrating inlet (b).
— Site is in an area of shoreline growth (accretion) or low shoreline erosion. Evidence of an eroding shoreline includes (a) sand bluff or dune scarp at back of beach, (b) stumps or peat exposed on beach, (c) slumped features such as trees, dunes, or man-made structures, (d) protective devices such as seawalls, groins, or pumped sand.
— Site is located on portion of a beach backed by salt marsh (b).
— Site is away from low, narrow portions of a beach (b).

— Site is in an area of no or low historic overwash (b).

— Site is in a vegetated area that suggests stability (b,bl).

— Site drains water readily (b,bl).

— Fresh groundwater supply is adequate and uncontaminated—
there is proper spacing between water wells and septic systems (b,bl).

— Soil and elevation are suitable for efficient septic tank operation (b,bl).

— No compactable layers such as peat are present in soil below
footings—site is not on a buried salt marsh (b).

— Adjacent structures are adequately spaced and of sound construction (b,bl).

— Site is fronted by salt marsh or stable bluff (bl).

Analysis of specific coastal regions: "safe," "caution," and "danger" zones

Virtually all sites along the coast are unique, and confidence in the
relative safety of a site is best established in the field by a qualified
geologist. The maps included in this section, thus, are generalized
with respect to relative safety within large regions and are accurate
only as a broad guide. More specific maps of the hazards along
Maine's large sand beaches may be obtained from the Maine
Geological Survey (see appendix B).

In considering the soundness of development in various coastal
regions of Maine, three categories of relative safety are defined.
"Danger" areas are those beaches or bluffs that are rapidly eroding or which have experienced problems in the recent past. Along
many beaches, such as portions of Old Orchard Beach, the danger
applies only to the first row of properties bordering the beach,
since more landward properties rarely experience storm damage.
Similarly, dangerously eroding bluffs are not dangerous to property hundreds of yards from the shoreline. "Caution" areas are
those beaches or bluffs that are retreating at relatively slow or un-
certain rates. A site visit is clearly advised prior to construction
in these regions. "Safe" areas are regions of bedrock cliffs, or of
bluffs protected by extensive salt marshes. Not all locations within
"safe" zones are truly safe, owing to the scale of the maps, and
problems with sewage disposal remain in even safe locations. In
the case of storms, certain precautions are advised for all areas
(see appendix A).

In addition to hazards along the coast, the maps also provide a
key to the geological environments present on the shoreline. Of
necessity, these are also generalized. Some areas are still too complex and a general unit entitled "very locally complex" is marked.
"Urban" is indicated on the environment key in areas where
natural environments have largely been obliterated by human
development.

Arcuate embayments

New Hampshire–York. The *arcuate embayments* coastal compartment is regionally characterized by prominent sandy beaches
protecting extensive salt marshes with occasional rocky headlands

between the barrier spits. The region from New Hampshire to York is one of the rockiest in the compartment and, as a result, one of the safest (fig. 4.7). Long stretches of coast in Kittery (Gerrish Island) and York Harbor are mapped as rocky cliffs with occasional gravel beaches. The cliff tops are largely settled with expensive private homes or motels (fig. 4.8), and the small gravel beach areas are protected by Maine's sand dune law.

Dangerous bluffs may exist along the Piscataqua River Estuary, but they are outside the area of mapping. Dangerous beaches include Seapoint and Crescent Beach in Kittery, as well as the beaches in York Beach. Crescent and Seapoint beaches are protected by the Coastal Barrier Resources Act (chapter 5) and are clearly marked by storm washovers on their marsh side. Seapoint is estimated to be retreating at 2 feet per year.

York Beach region. Long and Short Sands beaches in York are mapped as largely dangerous, even though no measure of shoreline retreat is available (fig. 4.9). These beaches have been heavily developed since the nineteenth century and have few natural components of a beach remaining (fig. 4.10). One significant area of caution exists at the southern end of Long Sands Beach. Here a mobile home park is perched atop a stabilized bluff of glacial gravel (fig. 4.11). Aside from eliminating one source of sand for the narrow beach, the riprapped bluff could one day fail and undermine the trailers. As in most other beach areas in Maine, the danger associated with living adjacent to the beach's seawall does not extend inland where high ground offers protection from storms.

Ogunquit Inlet to Wells Inlet. The Ogunquit and Wells barrier spits extend in opposite directions from a common headland at Moody Point (fig. 4.12). Although they are the longest pair of spits in Maine, they are among the most dangerous.

The Ogunquit Beach spit, which at first glance appears almost pristine, has been profoundly influenced by human development. It is reachable by car over the bridge near its inlet. At this least stable portion of the barrier, not only a bridge but a motel and municipal parking lot constrict the dynamics of the tidal inlet (fig. 4.13). The motel and lot have each been damaged in the past despite the protection afforded by their seawalls and will undoubtedly be influenced by the sea again.

Along the main axis of the barrier a well-vegetated dune thinly masks a Soil Conservation Service dike (fig. 3.3). This massive dike was built in 1974 to repair dunes that had been damaged by foot traffic and, presumably, to slow down the estimated 5.5-foot per year historic retreat of the beach. Despite objections by knowledgeable scientists, such as Ken Fink at the University of Maine, the core of most of the "dune" was filled with gravel and coarse sand. Unfortunately, this incompatible, coarse material will not behave like finer-grained windblown sand when storms begin to cut into the dunes in the future.

At the northern border of the town of Ogunquit intense development begins with the sewage treatment plant (fig. 4.14). This is arguably the most poorly sited structure on the Maine coast and will someday come to haunt the officials who located the smelly and expensive eyesore in the back dune area of the beach.

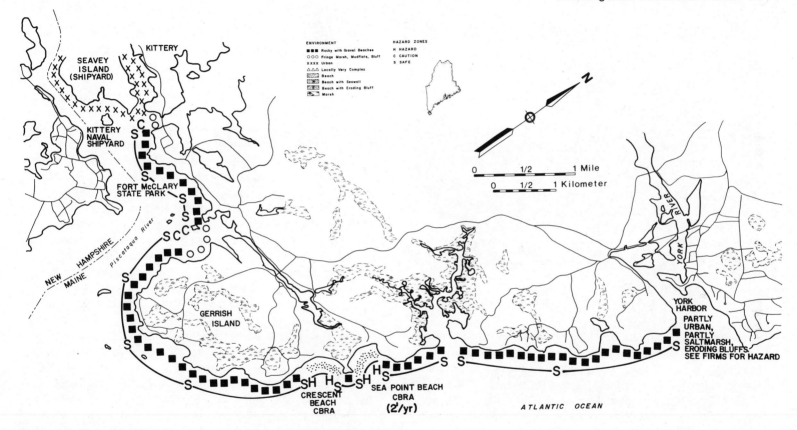

Figure 4.7. Site analysis of the southwestern Maine coast from New Hampshire to York Harbor.

Figure 4.8. Most of the safe, high rocky points on the southwestern coast are privately owned and covered with cottages and hotels.

Although protected by the Soil Conservation Service's dike/dune structure, the long-term future of the plant is questionable.

As one continues north of the sewage treatment plant, residential development, accompanied by seawalls, extends all the way to Wells Inlet (fig. 4.15). There are no active dunes left on Moody Beach, and a gravel ramp exists adjacent to many of the seawalls. Moody Beach is the site of a recent court case in which homeowners want to bar the public from "trespassing" on the beach for recreational purposes. Despite the deteriorated nature of Moody Beach, the case is important for establishing a precedent along much of the privately owned coast of Maine.

Freshwater tree stumps and salt marsh peat have been described from the low tide portions of Wells Beach and attest to the landward migration of that barrier spit. Despite an estimated cost of $20,000 per lot, new and larger seawalls to replace smaller structures damaged in the storms of 1986–87 were recently proposed to hold back the ocean at many locations along the beach. These have been rejected by the State Board of Environmental Protection but will undoubtedly be proposed after future damaging storms.

At the tidal inlet of the Webhannet River rock jetties built in the 1960s by the Corps of Engineers significantly interfere with the natural storage and movement of sand. Shoreline change maps record the growth of the beach on either side of the jetties where sand moving with the longshore current is impounded by the structures (figs. 3.2, 4.16). This sand is presumably derived from the nearby beaches, which have eroded and are now veneered with gravel.

Despite their impact on the adjacent beaches, the jetties have not functioned well, and there was recently a sand castle building contest held in the harbor, which has filled in. The in-filling at the harbor is no surprise to coastal geologists since it is located on the tidal delta of the inlet. To compound the problem, the sandy spoils from the original dredging were dumped on the salt marsh and are now viewed as potential development sites (fig. 3.2). The final chapter of how-not-to-build-soundly-on-the-coast has yet

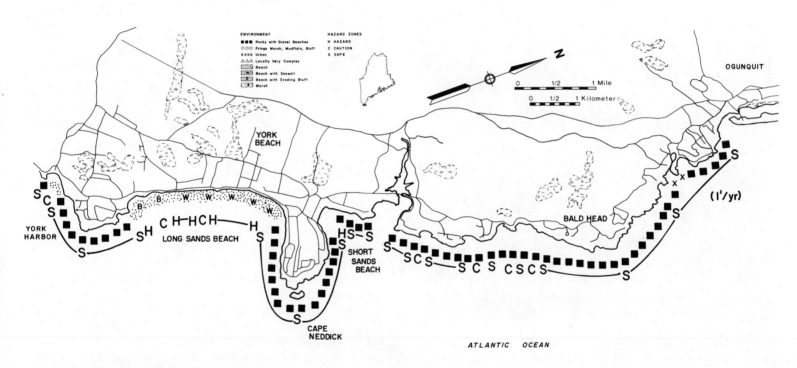

Figure 4.9. Site analysis of the York Beach region.

A

B

Figure 4.10. (a) View south along Long Sands Beach and (b) view east along Short Sands Beach. The lack of sand dunes in these developed areas renders them dangerous sites during storms.

Figure 4.11. This riprapped bluff in York Beach was the probable source of sand for the adjacent beaches. Despite the beach's engineered shoreline, slow retreat is likely.

to be written in Wells because no one is happy with the present situation. In the near future the Corps of Engineers must conduct maintenance dredging at the channel and anchorage or admit that the project is a failure. If they decide to dredge again, which is likely, they will hopefully locate a disposal site for the spoils (sand) within the beach system this time.

Drakes Island–Kennebunk River Inlet. Like many places in Maine, the coast from Drakes Island to the Kennebunk River Inlet is a mosaic of intensely developed and virtually pristine sites (fig. 4.17). Immediately adjacent to the Wells Inlet (fig. 3.2), the newly accreted beach is undeveloped and included in the Laud-

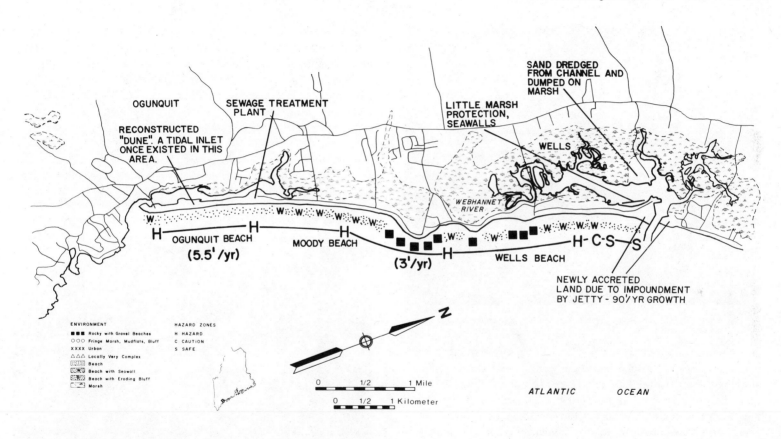

OGUNQUIT

SEWAGE TREATMENT PLANT

RECONSTRUCTED "DUNE". A TIDAL INLET ONCE EXISTED IN THIS AREA.

SAND DREDGED FROM CHANNEL AND DUMPED ON MARSH

LITTLE MARSH PROTECTION, SEAWALLS

WELLS

W W W W W W W

W H H H

W
OGUNQUIT BEACH
(5.5'/yr)

MOODY BEACH

WEBHANNET RIVER

W W W W W
W W
H

(3'/yr)

WELLS BEACH

H-C-S-S

NEWLY ACCRETED LAND DUE TO IMPOUNDMENT BY JETTY - 90'/YR GROWTH

ENVIRONMENT

■■■ Rocky with Gravel Beaches
○○○ Fringe Marsh, Mudflats, Bluff
XXXX Urban
△△△ Locally Very Complex
░░░ Beach
▒▒▒ Beach with Seawall
▓▓▓ Beach with Eroding Bluff
〰〰 Marsh

HAZARD ZONES

H HAZARD
C CAUTION
S SAFE

N

0   1/2   1 Mile

0   1/2   1 Kilometer

ATLANTIC   OCEAN

Figure 4.12. Site analysis of the Ogunquit to Wells Inlet area.

Figure 4.13. Unsafe development of the Ogunquit Beach spit.

holm Farm Estuarine Sanctuary. Proceeding north from this attractive lot, the scene changes dramatically (fig. 4.18). Houses built atop the former frontal dune ridge extend for about a mile and are protected by a continuous, though uneven seawall. Although this unwise development immediately adjacent to the now rocky beach is dangerous, as in other locations, the danger does not extend inland past the road. Although relatively safe from storms, the back-

barrier land that abuts the marshes of the Rachel Carson Preserve and Laudholm Estuarine Sanctuary, as well as the mainland abutting the salt marsh, are nonetheless poor sites for condominium or residential house construction. The development occurring in these areas now is robbing the marsh of an ecologically crucial edge, especially where the mowed lawns and floodlights extend to the very edge of the high tide boundary (fig. 4.19).

Figure 4.14. A poorly located sewage plant, parking lot, and numerous residences mark the change from relatively pristine Ogunquit Beach to highly altered Moody Beach. A historic inlet existed in this area, and a new one could form where the river (right) closely borders the back of Moody Beach.

Figure 4.15. A gravel ramp and seawalls in Moody Beach and Wells Beach mark the shoreline along Maine's most damaged section of "beach."

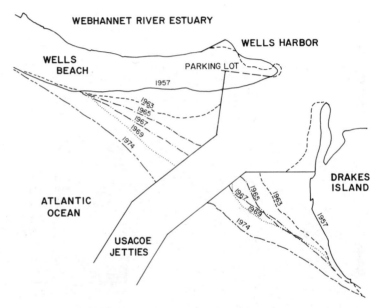

Figure 4.16. Shoreline change at Wells Inlet is a result of sediment trapping by the Army Corps of Engineers' jetties. Despite their impact on adjacent beaches, the jetties have not stopped sand from filling in the "harbor." (Modified from Timson and Kale, 1979.)

The Laudholm Farm Estuarine Sanctuary begins at the end of the developed road on Drakes Island and represents one of the only extensive undeveloped barrier beach/salt marsh areas in southern Maine with a tidal inlet. On the northern side of the Little River Inlet the double spit system of Crescent Surf and Parsons Beach continues as a relatively undeveloped extension of the estuarine sanctuary. After reaching a compromise with the state, the private owners of Crescent Surf recently agreed to restrict development to the relatively safe maritime forest extending

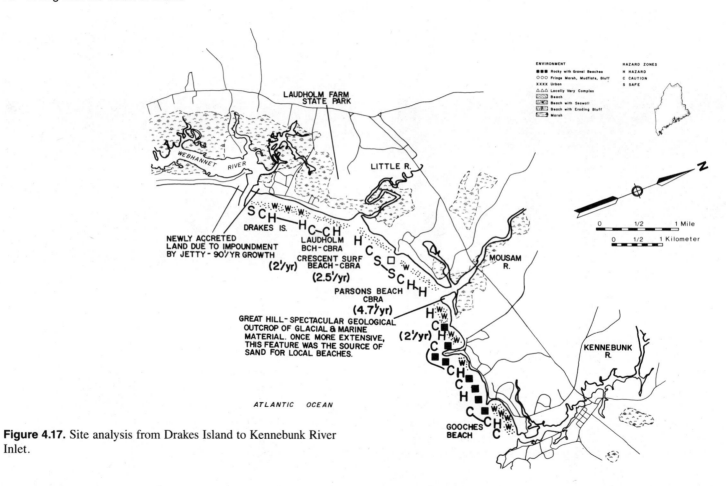

Figure 4.17. Site analysis from Drakes Island to Kennebunk River Inlet.

Figure 4.18. Construction of residences and seawalls on frontal dunes has robbed Drakes Island of the protection and beauty of a natural sand beach.

Figure 4.19. This overdeveloped southern Maine beach is trapped between rising water on both sides.

along the axis of the barrier (fig. 4.20). On Parsons Beach seawalls protect a couple of properties, while another was moved to the landward side of the barrier following the damaging storm of 1978.

On the northern side of the Mousam River inlet intense development resumes at Great Hill (fig. 2.7). This spectacular outcrop of glacial gravel and ocean mud represents the sort of deposits that eroded in the past to produce the beaches of the Wells Embayment. Regrettably, Great Hill is covered with residences today

and surrounded by a framework of rocks to prevent erosion of the valuable real estate (fig. 4.21).

North of Great Hill all the beaches extending to the Kennebunk River are backed by seawalls (cover photo). The landward areas here are somewhat dangerous since the seawalls have failed in the past and cannot continue to hold back the sea. The beaches are often rocky, and artificial nourishment may be the only remedy to return a sandy berm to this area.

Figure 4.20. Although this dune area once was scheduled to be covered with residences, the owners wisely reached an agreement with the state to locate development in the nearby maritime forest.

Cape Arundel to Fortunes Rocks. The stretch of coast from Cape Arundel to Fortunes Rocks consists of numerous islands and shoals, rocky headlands, sand beaches, salt marshes, and lagoons (fig. 4.22). In short, it is the most complex area in the arcuate embayments compartment.

Most of the region from the Kennebunk River to the Goose Rocks Beach consists of safe rocky points, but caution is indicated because erosion of bluffs and gravel beaches is reported from the area. Most of the seaward edge of Goose Rocks Beach is mapped as dangerous because construction is too close to the beach and seawalls interfere with the natural storage and movement of sand. While a small region of relative safety exists south of newly accreted land at the inlet of the Little River, numerous properties are dangerously sited too close to the unstable inlet itself.

Figure 4.21. Erosion of the glacial deposits at Great Hill, Kennebunkport, provided the sand that formed the beaches of the Wells Embayment. A cribwork of stones presently inhibits erosion of the hill, and a source of "new" sand for the region is lacking.

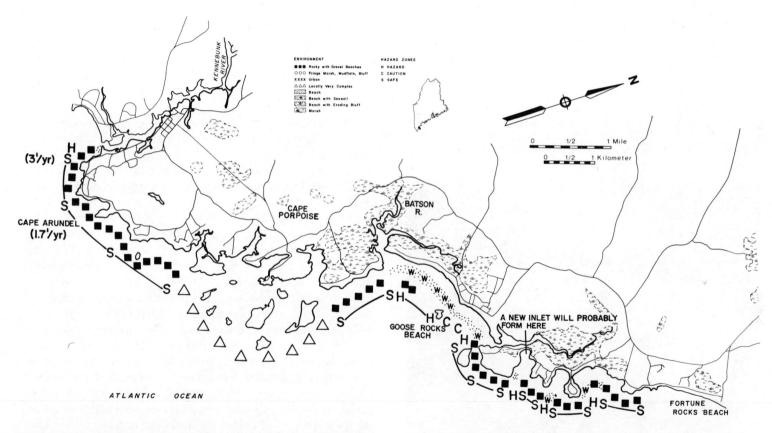

Figure 4.22. Site analysis from Cape Arundel to Fortunes Rocks.

From Goose Rocks to Biddeford safe rocky points are interspersed with dangerously eroding pocket beaches (fig. 2.2). The beach's landward migration is clearly indicated by washover deposits among the dunes and peat exposures on the lower beach. A new inlet will likely form at Curtis Cove when the narrow barrier is breached into the Little River (fig. 4.23).

Figure 4.23. A narrow beach with private road probably will be cut by a tidal inlet in the Kennebunk area.

Biddeford Pool. Biddeford Pool is a spectacular embayment protected from the open sea by Fletcher Neck, a tombolo, on its southern side and Hills Beach, a tombolo, to the north (fig. 4.24). A navigable inlet between Hills Beach and the rocky point of Biddeford Pool proper connects the embayment known as "The Pool" with the sea.

That Biddeford Pool was formed by the landward migration of barrier beaches, which derived their sand from glacial bluff erosion and the Saco River, was demonstrated by the research of Leita Hulmes, daughter of a local resident. The bay side of Fletcher Neck consists of washover or former inlet delta deposits now colonized by salt marsh. The ocean side of Fletcher Neck is almost completely lined with houses perched atop the former frontal dune ridge. Thus the processes that formed Fletcher Neck now threaten the properties located on it, and virtually the entire stretch of beach is mapped as dangerous despite protection from often massive seawalls (fig. 4.25). Storms will certainly wash away some of these houses in the future and a new inlet may someday form. At the eastern end of Fletcher Neck a tiny park, which charges a fee for nonresidents, offers the only public access to the beach. While it seems unfair to criticize the only publicly accessible beach in the area, the Biddeford beach offers an ironic environmental perspective to the visitor. Adjacent to the restrooms are signs warning the public to stay off the park's dunes at risk of a fine. Still farther seaward, however, a wooden bulkhead cuts off the natural supply of sand to the dunes and endangers the public beach seaward of it (fig. 4.26). Meanwhile, to the east, a pristine

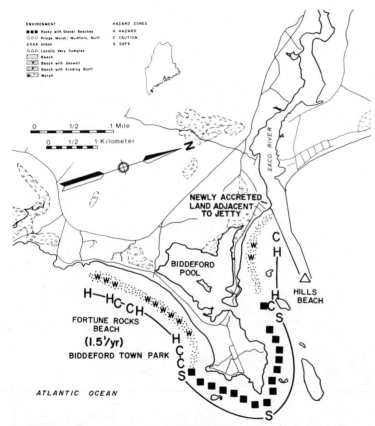

Figure 4.24. Site analysis of Biddeford Pool.

stretch of open beach owned by a convent shows what the natural beach could look like and where the natural dune line should be (landward of the seawall).

Hills Beach borders the northern side of The Pool and is sheltered by several small islands and a Corps of Engineers jetty. Nevertheless, houses are located dangerously close to the ocean along much of the beach and require protection from seawalls. On this narrow barrier beach even the landward side of the spit is considered dangerous because of flooding from The Pool. Only

Figure 4.25. Frontal dune development on the beach near Biddeford Pool. The dark band of seaweed indicates the narrow beach that exists at high tide. Note that natural dunes have retreated far landward of the seawall.

Figure 4.26. Dune trespassers are fined on the public beach near Biddeford Pool, yet a massive seawall cuts off the supply of sand and narrows the public beach.

in the shadow of the Saco River jetty has sufficient sand accreted to offer natural protection to dwellings.

Camp Ellis to Goosefare Brook. In the mid-nineteenth century the Corps of Engineers began to improve navigation on the then commercially important Saco River. The enormous sandbar at the mouth of the river was dredged, the river channel moved, and the

first of several jetty projects completed by the turn of the century. As a result of displacing the sandbar, the land at what is now Camp Ellis grew almost 700 feet seaward and was developed for residences (fig. 3.1). This was temporary growth resulting from disturbance of the existing sand deposits, however, and by 1909 the beach had retreated 600 feet (fig. 4.27). Since then seawalls have reflected wave energy and prevented sand from forming much of a beach in the Camp Ellis area; yet ironically the seawalls have offered little protection to the often-damaged properties remaining (fig. 3.10). Thus our map (fig. 4.28) shows this area to

Figure 4.27. Shoreline changes at Camp Ellis have resulted from human activity as well as geological processes. (Modified from an Army Corps of Engineers study, 1936.)

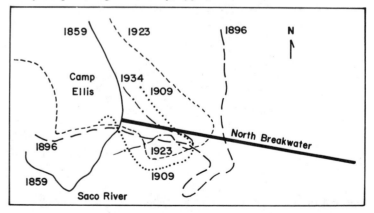

be dangerous, and it will remain so despite recent efforts to erect a more massive seawall from the jetty to Surf Street.

What remains of Surf Street exists only because of a massive, publicly subsidized seawall. Despite its size (figs. 4.29, 3.6), the wall is destroyed and rebuilt almost annually by the town of Saco to protect a handful of residences. The town recently requested that the Army build a "bigger, better wall," but the Corps of Engineers has wisely held back because of state regulations preventing such action as well as a knowledge that a bigger wall would destroy what little remains of the intertidal beach.

North of Camp Ellis, the beach remains steep, but houses are prudently set back behind frontal dunes and a safe, natural beach system exists. Ferry Beach State Park is centrally located in this area and offers the visitor access to the sea and a feeling of what all of Saco Bay was once like (fig. 1.11B).

From Kinney Shores to Goosefare Brook, residential development creeps back out of the safe maritime forest to the frontal dune, and dangerous sites abound. This overdeveloped stretch of land was hit hard by the 1978 storm (fig. 4.30) and will be damaged again where seawalls and houses have damaged or eliminated the natural beach-dune system.

Old Orchard Beach: Goosefare Brook to Scarborough Town Line. Goosefare Brook was named in colonial times for the migratory birds that used the small marsh as a refuge. The brook has been deleteriously affected by people in recent years, however.

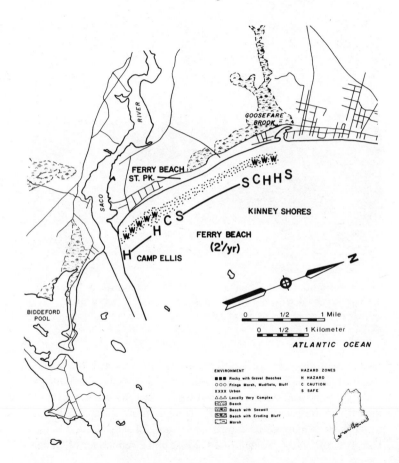

Figure 4.28. Site analysis from Camp Ellis to Goosefare Brook.

A

B

Figure 4.29. (a) The typical condition of Surf Street, Saco, following the winter storm season; (b) despite the large size of the wall (fig. 3.6) and its damage to the adjacent beach, storms each year still manage to undermine the road and threaten property.

As the dumping spot for Old Orchard's treated sewage, the water quality of the brook is low. The inlet was stabilized on its north end by a bulkhead when a railroad line crossed the stream around the turn of the century (fig. 4.31). The beach immediately adjacent to the inlet is mapped as dangerous because of seawalls and house construction on the frontal dunes. Most of the remainder of Ocean Park, though densely settled, is mapped as a safe or caution zone because of the substantial sand dunes protecting the properties (fig. 4.32). These dunes were begun by local efforts after the damaging storm of 1978, and although partly weakened by the recent emplacement of two sewer pipes in their core, the dunes will offer significant protection against future storms.

As one approaches the pier in central Old Orchard, the quality of the beach system declines and the danger to shorefront properties increases (fig. 4.33). Heavy pedestrian traffic coupled with a bulldozing effort prevents sand dunes from forming along a considerable stretch of Grand Beach (fig. 1.3A). In most places

Figure 4.30. Storm damage at Kinney Shores following the 1978 storm. Maine Geological Survey file photo.

Figure 4.31. Goosefare Brook and its tidal delta in 1970. Note the former inner channel near Kinney Shores (left) as well as the railroad trestle crossing the brook. This dynamic tidal inlet is highly unstable. Photo by Stewart Farrell.

motels, restaurants, and more recently condominiums have been constructed on the remnants of the frontal dunes. There has been talk of creating artificial dunes along parts of this beach to protect properties, but sand dunes do not fare well in the high velocity flood hazard zone of the beach where they may be located. The safest plan for this area would locate all future construction projects on the landward side of Grand Avenue and reestablish natural dunes along the former dune ridge. Local promoters of development would prefer a row of high rises without even consid-

ering where the future shoreline will be or what the beach may come to look like (fig. 4.34). Decisions will soon be made that will determine whether Old Orchard is developed soundly, preserving the finest beach in the state, or whether the entire area evolves into another Miami Beach(less).

As one moves toward the Scarborough town line, the urbanized shoreline of the Old Orchard pier area becomes more suburban.

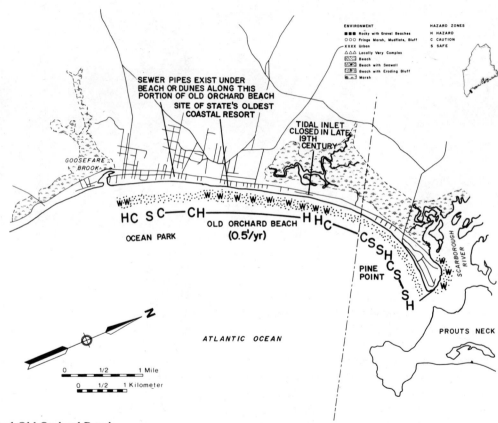

Figure 4.32. Site analysis of central Old Orchard Beach.

Figure 4.33. With a highly developed shorefront, including seawalls and high-rise condominiums and no natural dune system, central Old Orchard Beach may be an expensive problem following future winter storms.

The trend in recent years has been to replace the graceful old estates with condominiums (fig. 4.35). The problem with this is that large volumes of sand, which the beach will need to naturally replenish itself in the future, are buried beneath huge, immobile, relatively indestructible buildings and parking lots. Near the site

of a former tidal inlet developers recently proposed to build the highest building in Maine. This has led to a public outcry against high-rise buildings on beaches, and new regulations by the state's Department of Environmental Protection (chapter 5).

Pine Point to Prouts Neck. In the 1960s the Army Corps of Engineers constructed a jetty at the mouth of the Scarborough River to improve "commercial" navigation. The dredged spoils were partly dumped on Pine Point, and development of this spit end began in earnest (figs. 4.36, 2.17B). Meanwhile, the jetty impounded sand moving northward with the prevailing longshore current, and the beach began to grow adjacent to the jetty as it had in Wells (fig. 3.2). It is because of this growth that much of Pine Point's ocean side is mapped "safe" (figs. 4.32, 4.37). Even newly constructed residences are far from the sea today and protected by large, healthy dunes.

The same jetty that led to beach growth on the ocean side of Pine Point cut off the sand supply to the bay side of the spit. A much-debated seawall was permitted to protect eroding properties here only after an amendment was passed by the legislature (fig. 4.38). The entire back side of Pine Point remains dangerous despite seawall protection.

On the north side of the Scarborough River, Ferry Beach and Western Beach are still in nearly pristine condition. An exclusive golf course presently prevents development behind Western Beach, and Ferry Beach is now a Scarborough town park. Each of these beaches has eroded and grown in the recent past as a result of interference with the sand supply to the south. Plans to expand

A

B

Figure 4.34. (a) The first high-rise condominium was constructed at Old Orchard Beach in 1984. More have subsequently been built. (b) When will Maine's finest beach come to resemble Virginia Beach?

the anchorage near Pine Point run the risk of further disrupting the supply of sand needed by these beaches and the adjacent Scarborough Marsh.

Prouts Neck to Cape Elizabeth. Between Prouts Neck and Cape Elizabeth there are numerous sand beaches and rocky points (fig. 4.39). The rocky points are private refuges for the wealthy and are the safest locations to build in the area. The sand beaches vary from safe to extremely dangerous.

Scarborough Beach is publicly accessible through the state park entrance. A maritime forest is safely tucked behind substantial dunes along most of this beach. Higgens Beach, in contrast, is privately owned and has been largely destroyed. A seawall protecting the road has robbed the beach of its sand (fig. 4.40), which has apparently moved to the north with the longshore current (fig. 4.41). An old hotel was recently destroyed by a storm along this beach, and numerous properties near the Spurwink River are in serious danger of future erosion.

The remaining beaches in this section of the coast are mapped as caution zones (fig. 4.39). Some of these are not publicly accessible but probably have much in common with Crescent Beach

Figure 4.35. A new condominium abuts the graceful old Danton estate on Old Orchard Beach (above). A plan to replace the Danton house with a massive high-rise condo continues the unsound development trend along this portion of the beach.

Figure 4.36. Development of Pine Point has followed a predictable path (right). Beginning in the 1960s the Army Corps of Engineers built a jetty to assist commercial navigation. The dredged spoils were partly dumped on Pine Point, and residential development followed in the 1970s (this photo). Residential development is now 100 percent complete, and commercial development is creeping in (often contrary to local wishes). Now the town of Scarborough has requested that the Corps of Engineers expand the anchorage, presumably for pleasure boats. Are condos next? Photo by Stewart Farrell.

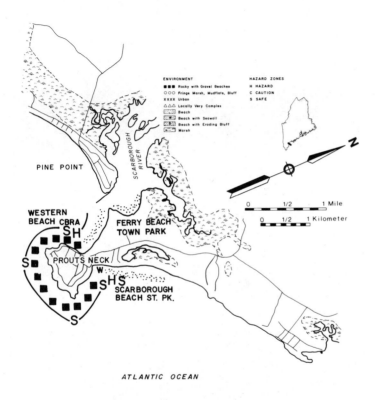

ENVIRONMENT

■■■ Rocky with Gravel Beaches
OOO Fringe Marsh, Mudflats, Bluff
XXXX Urban
△△△ Locally Very Complex
▢▢ Beach
▨▨ Beach with Seawall
▨▨ Beach with Eroding Bluff
↔ Marsh

HAZARD ZONES

H HAZARD
C CAUTION
S SAFE

PINE POINT

SCARBOROUGH RIVER

WESTERN
BEACH CBRA
■S H

FERRY BEACH
TOWN PARK

S

PROUTS NECK

■W

■SHS

■SHS

SCARBOROUGH
BEACH ST. PK.

S

ATLANTIC OCEAN

0   1/2   1 Mile

0   1/2   1 Kilometer

Figure 4.37. Site analysis of Pine Point to Prouts Neck.

Figure 4.38. Seawall construction at Pine Point was permitted by a special amendment to the Sand Dune Law despite two denials by the State Board of Environmental Protection.

State Park. The beaches are made of sand and gravel and have no obvious source of new sediment. Construction along these beaches should be considered only in the upland areas behind all dune and wetland regions.

Indented shoreline compartment

Western Casco Bay: Cape Elizabeth to the Presumpscot River.
The geological character of the shoreline changes profoundly as

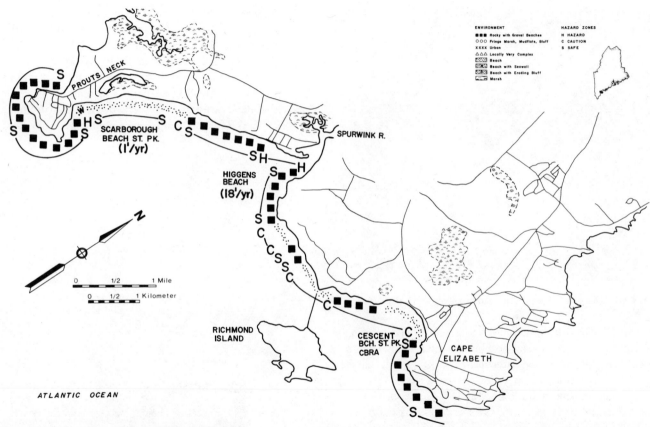

ENVIRONMENT
- ■■ Rocky with Gravel Beaches
- ○○○ Fringe Marsh, Mudflats, Bluff
- ×××× Urban
- △△△ Locally Very Complex
- Beach
- Beach with Seawall
- Beach with Eroding Bluff
- Marsh

HAZARD ZONES
H HAZARD
C CAUTION
S SAFE

PROUTS NECK

SCARBOROUGH
BEACH ST. PK.
(1'/yr)

SPURWINK R.

HIGGENS
BEACH
(18'/yr)

RICHMOND
ISLAND

CESCENT
BCH. ST. PK.
CBRA

CAPE
ELIZABETH

ATLANTIC   OCEAN

N

0   1/2   1 Mile

0   1/2   1 Kilometer

Figure 4.39. Site analysis from Prouts Neck to Cape Elizabeth.

Figure 4.40. Higgens Beach today remains overdeveloped.

one leaves Saco Bay by rounding Cape Elizabeth and entering Casco Bay (fig. 4.42). Barrier beaches are replaced by an almost continuous rocky shore, and extensive back-barrier salt marshes, such as in the Scarborough River, are matched by mud flats with small fringing marshes and eroding bluffs. The reasons for the abrupt change in the shape of the coast are complex but probably have to do with rivers earlier in the geological history of the bays.

Where Saco Bay has received thousands of years of sand from the Saco River, Casco Bay gets only meager amounts of mud from its small rivers, the Fore, Presumpscot, Royal, and Cousins.

The Cape Elizabeth coast is largely privately owned and inaccessible to the public. At Cape Elizabeth Light (Two Lights) and Portland Head Light parking is permitted and the character of the coast may be discerned. Here, low to moderate cliffs of Casco Bay's ancient bedrock dominate the coast. Little or no

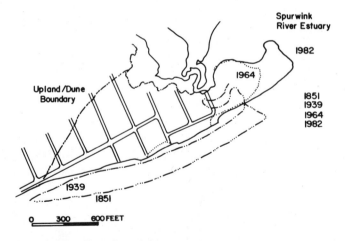

Figure 4.41. Shoreline change map for Higgens Beach. (Modified from Timson and Lerman, 1979.)

unconsolidated sand and mud are seen on the rocks, and future development of this rocky shoreline will require proper sewage treatment instead of the formerly common overboard pipe leading from bathroom to sea. Indentations in the coast occur where weaker rocks were more deeply eroded by glaciers and small valleys were filled with gravel and sand. Erosion of these small deposits has formed numerous sand, gravel, and boulder beaches. Where seawalls presently protect glacial bluffs from erosion, sediment-starved beaches will slowly become rocky boulder ramps (fig. 4.43). The largest beach in Casco Bay, Willard Beach, nicely illustrates the sand-starved nature of Casco Bay's small "pocket" beaches (fig. 2.13). Willard Beach is in South Portland (fig. 4.43) and tucked, like a pocket, between two rocky promontories. A deep commercial channel exists seaward of its broad low-tide terrace and sloping sand and gravel beach. Although the cove was probably used only by fishermen in colonial times, Willard Beach was popular for swimming until closed by pollution in the 1950s. Cleaner water resulting from better sewage disposal led to increased use of the beach in the 1980s, along with a perception that it was eroding. The Corps of Engineers estimated a retreat rate of 1 to 2 feet per year for the beach in the past century, attributable in part to sea level rise and in part to seawalls constructed in front of a few cottages. Since seawalls have cut off the only obvious sources of new sand to the beach at the eastern and western ends, the Corps of Engineers proposed to nourish the beach with material quarried from a nearby gravel pit. In addition, the Corps wanted

to construct an expensive seawall and groin system to retain the sand. Ironically, the same private development that walled off new sources of bluff sand would have benefited most from the Army Corps of Engineers' beach. Since protecting private property is a lower priority for the Corps than public land, the city of South Portland was to pay $500,000 for their share of the new beach as well as the perpetual costs of maintenance. This was more than the city could afford, and Willard Beach remains a narrow beach at high tide and a dangerous site for construction (fig. 4.42).

The Fore River separates Portland and South Portland and is a totally urbanized estuary for most of its length. Although mud flats with fringing marshes are reclaiming abandoned industrialized areas in places, condominiums are quickly springing up on both sides of the Fore River mouth.

Urbanization continues along the base of Portland's Eastern Promenade, a hill of glacial material. Enough sediment formerly eroded from bluffs at the base of the hill to provide sand for East End Beach. Riprap to protect a railroad line and sewage treatment plant ended bluff erosion, and East End Beach is a narrow, steep beach today. Rock walls continue beneath Tukey's Bridge, and all of the Back Bay shore is man-made. Most of the flat eastern side of the bay is filled land for a considerable distance inland from I-295. A high, wave-cut cliff exists along most of the city side of the bay, and Deering Oaks Duck Pond was a salt marsh creek in the nineteenth century. Salt marsh has recently been planted along most of Baxter Boulevard to provide cover for migrating

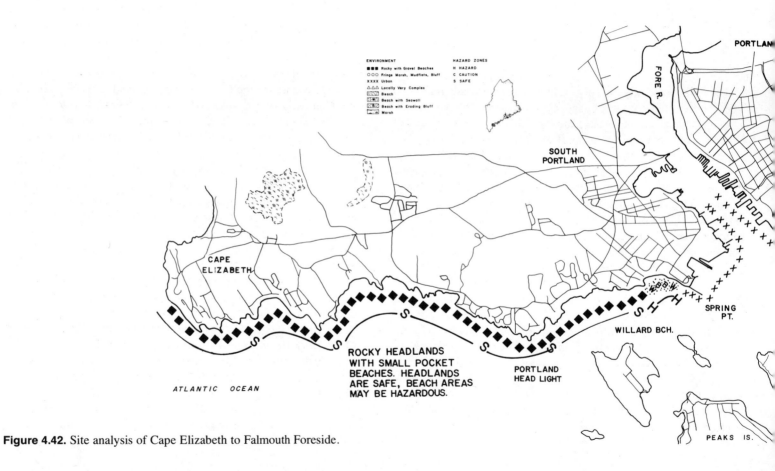

Figure 4.42. Site analysis of Cape Elizabeth to Falmouth Foreside.

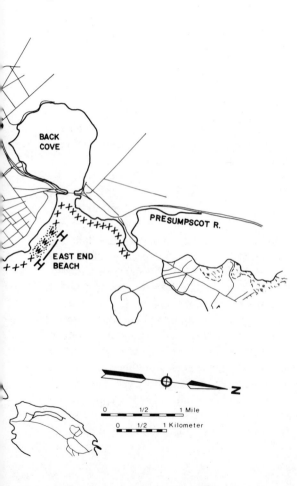

BACK
COVE

PRESUMPSCOT R.

EAST END
BEACH

0   1/2   1 Mile

0   1/2   1 Kilometer

waterfowl. Prior to development, the steep hill that fronts most
of the western side of Back Bay was an eroding bluff that fed a
natural marsh system.

From Tukey's Bridge to Martin Point Bridge much of the shoreline is urbanized, and seawalls protect the base of all railroad and
automobile bridges as well as the industrial and medical com-
plexes in the area. Despite their protection, slope failure remains
a potential problem along this area.

Presumpscot River to the Harraseeket River. The suburban
stretch of coast from the Presumpscot River to the Harraseeket
River is one of the most dangerously developed portions of Casco
Bay (fig. 4.44). Much of the shoreline is supported by bluffs of
sand or mud and is prone to chronic erosion due to slumping
(fig. 4.45). Along the estuary of the Presumpscot River, rapid bluff
erosion may be observed at Gilsland Farm, home of the Maine
Audubon Society, due to channel migration by the river. Along
the coast of Falmouth Foreside the erosion is attributable to wave
attack from the sea and groundwater undercutting of bluffs. The
authors have measured retreat rates up to 3 feet per year at numerous locations along this coast, and more rapid rates may occur
during sudden slope failures. Such large slope failures might
occur in areas like the Town Landing and Casco Terrace because
of the steep slope of the land surface toward the sea and the unconsolidated nature of the land. The clearing away of vegetation to
improve coastal views or the dumping of gravel or vegetation on
the eroding bluffs, as are common in the area, serve to increase the
threat of erosion rather than inhibit it.

Figure 4.43. Pocket beaches in Cape Elizabeth.

Along the tidal portions of the Royal, Cousins, and Harraseeket rivers increasingly large numbers of pleasure boats have led to new marine construction and necessitated frequent dredging of channels (fig. 4.46). One problem associated with the dredging can occur when it oversteepens a valley slope and leads to slumping. Removal of large quantities of mud can also deprive salt marsh and clam flat communities of the material they need to keep pace with rising sea level.

Eastern Casco Bay: Wolf Neck to Harpswell Neck. At the opposite end of Casco Bay from Portland the shoreline in many places appears as unaffected by development as portions of the Washington County coast. Suburban development associated with the growth of Freeport and Brunswick is threatening to alter the character as well as the quality of the coastal environment here, however. The unstable mainland coast along the western part of Maquoit Bay and Little Flying Point is especially susceptible to rapid deterioration (fig. 4.47). Bluff erosion rates greater than 3 feet per year have been measured here, and large landslides are common in some places (fig. 4.48). Within historic times great changes have occurred in some areas. The many "mast landings," or small colonial harbors used to export timber, have all filled in with mud flats or salt marshes. The source of much of the mud is eroding bluffs of Ice Age mud that must have retreated rapidly after being deforested in the eighteenth century. British charts show a location like Little Flying Point as a peninsula, when today it is virtually an island due to bluff retreat. Though bluff retreat, like beach migration, appears to be a widespread new "problem" today, prior to construction of residences shoreline migration was the natural response of the coast to rising sea level. Thus the great cost, ineffectiveness, and generally unsightly appearance of seawalls to hold back bluffs often make them unattractive solutions to the problems caused by locating houses too close to an eroding bluff.

Merepoint Neck, Harpswell Neck, and adjacent islands appear much safer for residential construction than the mainland coast just described (fig. 4.47). Here, adjacent to relatively deep channels, most of the bluffs of mud and sand already have fallen into the sea, and firm bedrock outcrops are common along the shore. While it is difficult to evaluate in detail this very private and relatively inaccessible region, dangerous sites are probably restricted to small coves where eroding bluffs still supply sediment to small marshes, flats, or beaches. Along with the safety of living on bedrock come the problems of water supply and sewage disposal. Because of lack of soil and proximity to salt water, it is often difficult to obtain a reliable freshwater supply on a small coastal lot. Overboard discharge of poorly treated sewage quickly renders local clam flats "polluted," and new development can often end traditional practices.

The large islands of Casco Bay. Because they are privately owned, and not publicly accessible, most of Casco Bay's small islands cannot be included on the site analysis map (fig. 4.49). The large islands vary greatly in accessibility from Cousins Island, which is easily reached by car, to Jewell Island, which must be visited by private boat.

Most of the islands that are exposed to ocean storms and adjacent to deep water have much in common with the outer portion of the Harpswell Neck and vicinity. Almost all of the coast of Jewell, Cushing, and Cliff islands, and much of Littlejohn, Peaks, Long, Chebeague, and Great Diamond are rocky and relatively safe for development (fig. 4.49). Dangerous areas are conspicuous, how-

ever, and beaches where caution is advised are prominent on Cliff, Chebeague, Little Chebeague, and Long islands. Some of these are protected by the Coastal Barrier Resources Act, and, without a doubt, all are eroding (figs. 4.50, 4.51). Most are cut off from new supplies of sand and are too remote for artificial nourishment to ever assist. Some beaches are backed by dangerously eroding bluffs on the landward sides of Long and Chebeague islands. These areas share the same dangers as those described for the mainland coast, and houses ought to be set back well away from bluff margins.

Maine's shoreline north and east of Casco Bay. While it is not possible at present to provide detailed site-analysis maps for the remainder of the Maine coast, several areas of important geological activity will be discussed. These are coastal locations that have figured prominently in recent media reports on coastal erosion and are experiencing great development pressure, and areas that have come to the authors' attention during recent research projects. Although the changes occurring at Popham Beach are probably unique to that location at the mouth of the state's largest river, the dynamics of shoreline change in Rockland and Lubec may be typical of large stretches of Maine's still-undeveloped "downeast coast."

Site analysis of Popham, Hunnewell, and Small Point beaches. While visitors to Maine commonly see Popham Beach State Park, this beach is only a small part of a much larger nearshore system that exists at the mouth of the Kennebec River. Other important sandy components to the system include privately owned, but

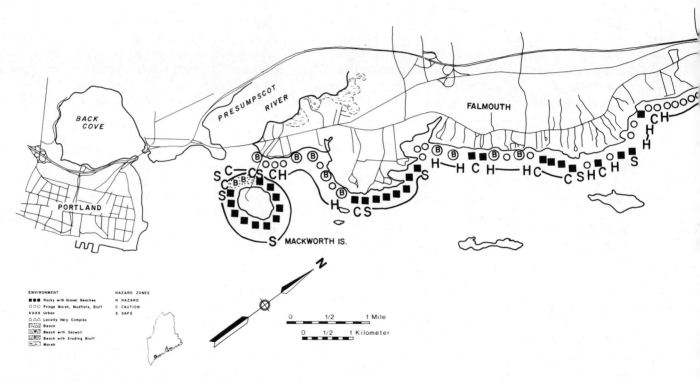

Figure 4.44. Site analysis of the Presumpscot River to the Harrasekett River.

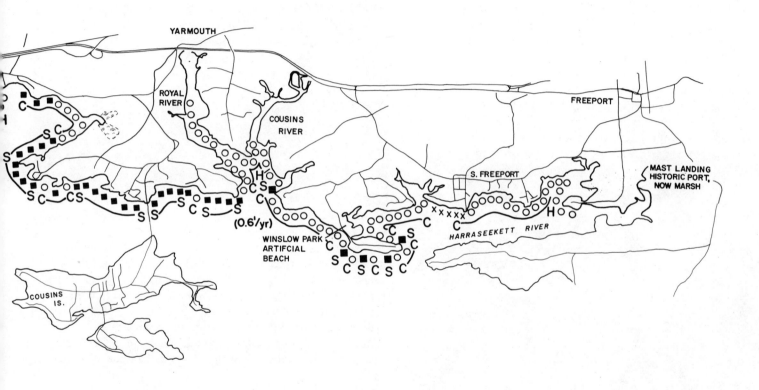

accessible, Small Point Beach, as well as the channel bottom of the Kennebec River and the offshore waters. Reid Beach State Park to the north is presently cut off from Popham Beach but shares a common geological origin.

The sand that moves about along these coastal environments is ultimately derived from the Kennebec River. Recent studies by Dan Belknap and other scientists from the University of Maine

Figure 4.46. Dredging near salt marshes on the Royal River.

Figure 4.45. If the salt marsh erodes, the bluffs soon follow.

indicate that when sea level fell about 9,000 years ago, the Kennebec deposited a large sandy delta seaward of its present mouth. As sea level has risen, this sand has been reworked to form the present beach systems of the area. It has been speculated by some that the Kennebec River continues to bring sand to the coast. While this may be true during extreme floods, recent research indicates that sand is tidally drawn into and up the Kennebec as far as Bath.

Figure 4.47. Site analysis of eastern Casco Bay: Wolf Neck to Harpswell Neck.

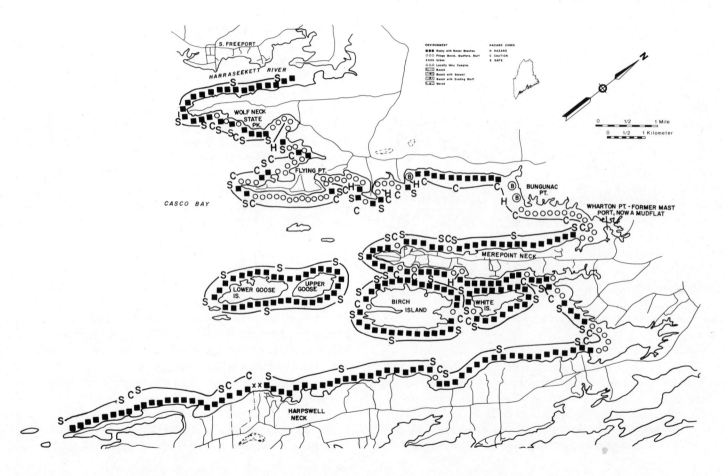

S. FREEPORT

HARRASEEKETT RIVER

WOLF NECK
STATE
PK.

FLYING PT.

CASCO BAY

BUNGUNAC
PT.

WHARTON PT. - FORMER MAST
PORT, NOW A MUDFLAT

MEREPOINT NECK

UPPER
GOOSE

LOWER GOOSE
IS.

BIRCH
ISLAND

WHITE
IS.

HARPSWELL
NECK

ENVIRONMENT

Rocky with Gravel Beaches
Fringe Marsh, Mudflats, Bluff
Urban
Locally Very Complex
Beach
Beach with Seawall
Beach with Eroding Bluff
Marsh

HAZARD ZONES

H HAZARD
C CAUTION
S SAFE

0   1/2   1 Mile
0   1/2   1 Kilometer

Figure 4.48. Landslides are common in eastern Casco Bay.

The site map (fig. 4.52) indicates that most of the Popham Beach system is dangerous for shoreline development. More properties have been lost on this beach in the past 15 years than in any other coastal area in Maine. The primary reason for property loss is shoreline fluctuation along Hunnewell Beach (fig. 4.53). This area has advanced and retreated significant distances in the past century, and lots developed during periods of growth have disappeared following periods of erosion (figs. 1.13, 4.3, 4.5). Because of the unstable nature of the beach, the State Board of Environmental Protection recently demanded the removal of one cottage that was rebuilt on the ruins of a former structure. The Maine Supreme Court upheld the decision and stated that the owner need not be compensated by the state for loss of property rights. This landmark decision has cooled development interest in the frontal dune areas of Popham Beach, and some structures have recently been moved landward (fig. 4.54).

The stretch of beach along the Kennebec River, which is locally known as Coast Guard Beach, is mapped as a caution zone (fig. 4.52). This is because the shoreline is more sheltered here, and a significant frontal dune line protects most of the properties.

Island-bay complex

Site analysis of Rockland Harbor area. Rockland Harbor is the first major embayment on the western shore of Penobscot Bay (fig. 4.55). Because of the exposed nature of outer Penobscot Bay, a large breakwater was constructed across the northern half of the harbor to block waves (fig. 4.56). While the structure undoubtedly serves that purpose well, it does little to alleviate bluff erosion on the nearby shoreline and may locally exacerbate the problem. Fortunately, a large resort complex has created a golf course where erosion is greatest, near the breakwater (fig. 4.56). This is wise coastal land use because as the bluffs erode the course hazard may increase, but the hazard to property remains distant.

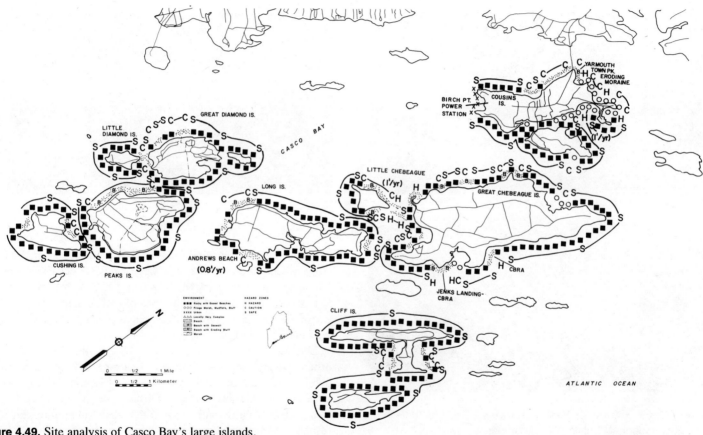

Figure 4.49. Site analysis of Casco Bay's large islands.

Figure 4.50. (a) Outwash on Jenks Beach with eroding bluffs; (b) eroding tombolo at Indian Point, Chebeague Island.

Figure 4.51. Mapped as "safe," this portion of Chebeague Island has hazardous beaches too small to map.

Along the inner, northern side of the harbor the hazard of bluff erosion is not remote. In 1973 a large landslide occurred here and threatened local property (fig. 4.57). Even now, erosion continues to scallop the shoreline into a series of embayments (fig. 4.56). Erosion is slowest where bedrock outcrops support the eroding Ice Age mud deposit.

Like most harbors, a significant portion of the Rockland area is urbanized and therefore of unknown hazard. Within part of this urbanized region the U.S. Army Corps of Engineers proposed construction and nourishment of a sandy beach. In the absence of a nearby eroding bluff of sand, this plan will require perpetual resupply from a local gravel pit.

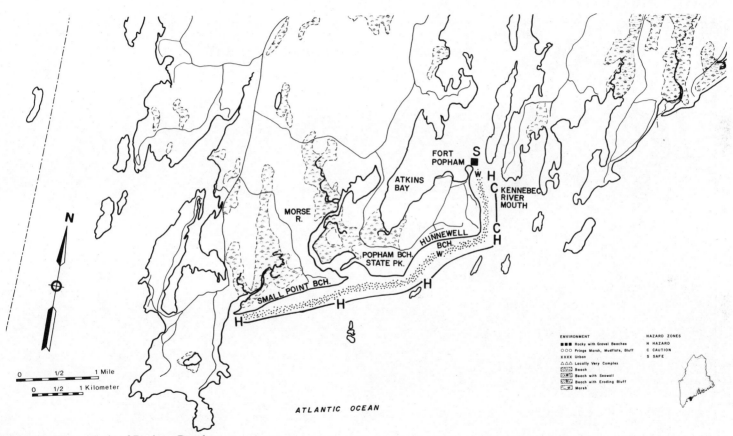

Figure 4.52. Site analysis of Popham Beach.

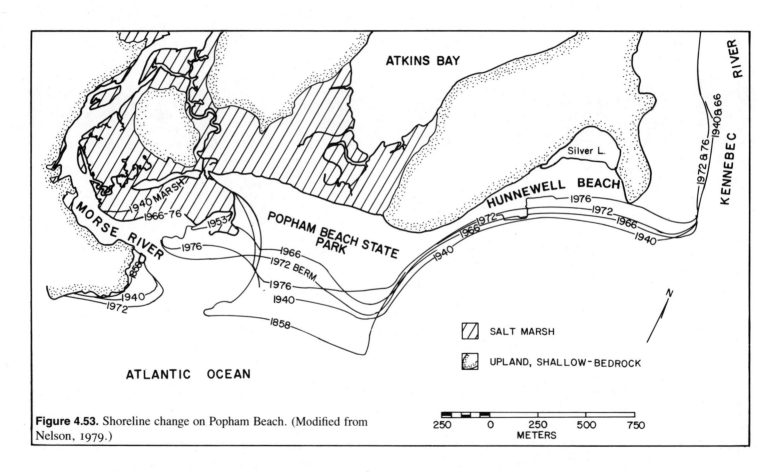

Figure 4.53. Shoreline change on Popham Beach. (Modified from Nelson, 1979.)

Figure 4.54. Hunnewell Beach (1987) with the Kennebec River in the background. Many houses have been lost and moved landward in this area; more will follow suit after future storms.

The southern portion of the harbor has several spots where local bluff erosion is a problem. It is more naturally sheltered than the other end of the embayment, however, and quite a bit rockier. It is mapped as a caution zone, and the most dangerous places occur where eroding bluffs are fronted by narrow sand or gravel beaches.

Riprapping of bluffs here, as elsewhere, will not enhance the safety of a property. Instead, a seawall will cut off the supply of material to the nearby beach or marsh and result in greater wave and tidal energy acting on the shoreline.

Cliffed shoreline compartment

Site analysis of the Lubec area. Between the town of Lubec and rocky West Quoddy Head stretches one of the most extraordinary portions of the Maine coast (fig. 4.58). The tidal range here is the greatest in the lower 48 states and reaches more than 25 feet several times per month. This is also within an area that repeated resurveys indicate is sinking rapidly. Published estimates of the rate of land subsidence suggest it has been as great as 9 millimeters per year between 1942 and 1966 and is probably caused by the earthquakes that frequently rock the area.

Regardless of the origin of the local subsidence, one outcome of it is rapid shoreline change (fig. 4.59). All of the bluffs of Ice Age mud in the embayment are eroding rapidly except where bedrock supports the bluff. This erosion renders all of the shoreline from the town of Lubec to West Quoddy Head a danger zone (fig. 4.58). Where small streams reach the coast, barrier beaches lie seaward of small marshes. These are no less dangerous areas than the eroding bluffs, and salt marsh peat on the seaward side of some beaches testifies to their rapid landward movement as well.

At the southern end of the embayment a large sand and gravel barrier and a complex cobble and boulder spit converge toward an

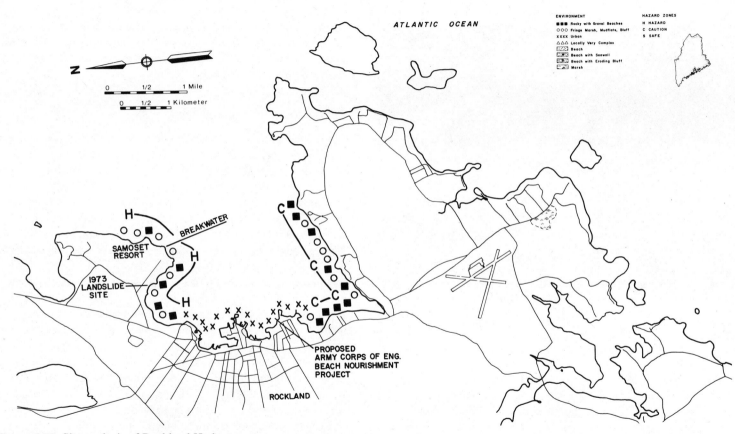

Figure 4.55. Site analysis of Rockland Harbor.

Figure 4.56. Bluff erosion has shaped the scalloped shoreline of Rockland. Trees line dangerous bluffs where historic landslides have occurred. Breakwater in the background abuts the Samoset Resort's golf course.

eroding heath, or raised freshwater wetland. An analysis of historic maps of this area reveals that the two beach areas began to evolve into their present form around the time of the Civil War (fig. 4.59). Prior to that, other barrier features existed seaward of the present coast and were destroyed as sea level rose in the region. Clearly these coastal regions are too dangerous for any sort of permanent structures. It is interesting to note that one of the first topographic maps of the region shows a fish factory and several buildings on

one gravel spit where now only posts protrude from the beach. During the winter a thick layer of ice covers much of the intertidal area, and large blocks of ice litter even the highest dunes on the beach. In this easternmost portion of Maine, extreme coastal conditions resulting from the local tidal regime, meteorological conditions, and regional subsidence make occupation of coastal sites by people dangerous in all locations except for the high, rocky cliffs.

Figure 4.57. A landslide in 1973 startled Rockland residents. The Ice Age mud deposit overturned trees but did not reach buildings seen in the background.

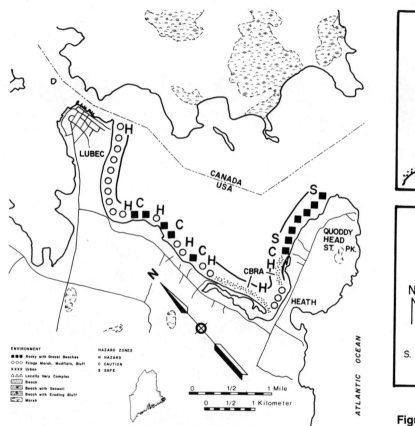

Figure 4.58. Site analysis of the Lubec area.

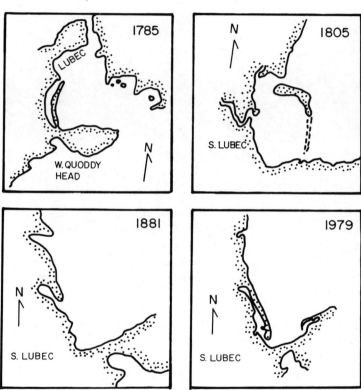

Figure 4.59. Shoreline change in the Lubec area. (Modified from Walsh, 1988.)

5 Coastal land use and the law in Maine

Since the early days of European colonization the inhabitants of Maine have shared a healthy respect for the dangers associated with the ocean. Experience demonstrated and common sense dictated that sand beaches were too dangerous to build permanent homes on, and salt marshes were too valuable to be developed for businesses or harbors. Unlike many states to the south, Maine's coast possesses a large number of high, rocky promontories and snug, protected harbors suitable for safe construction. In the years since World War II, however, growing population pressure and personal mobility have brought increasing numbers of "summer people" to the Maine coast. Finding many of the best and safest places already occupied, they have joined large numbers of local people in constructing vacation cottages and permanent homes on the dynamic sand beaches and eroding bluffs of Maine. During the same period, conservation groups have begun to promote regulation of coastal development and to simultaneously purchase environmentally significant parcels of coastal property for protection. In 1987 the people of Maine voted to purchase $35 million worth of new public land, some of it coastal. Still, in light of the fact that 97 percent of the Maine shore is privately owned (fig. 5.1), the future of the coastline, whether toward development or preservation, will be greatly influenced by the action of private citizens and their communities.

As noted in previous chapters, coastal environments are dynamic systems. Our philosophy on shoreline development is that land use should be in harmony with the natural processes that make up these systems. Various segments of society view the coastal zone differently and as a result hold different philosophies of land use. The extremes range from that of untouched preservationism to that of total unplanned urbanization. In some of our parks and major coastal resorts the extreme views have prevailed. But along most of the coast the cost of outright acquisition for preservation or of construction and maintenance for urban recreation cannot be met. It is here, on the greater part of the coast, that multiple land uses and protection of the environment must go hand in hand. For this reason the function of state government has been mediation between groups with conflicting goals by enacting compromise legislation. Current and prospective owners of coastal property should be aware of their responsibilities under current law with respect to development and land use.

Below is a list of current land-use regulations applicable to the Maine coast. The explanations we have provided are general; Appendix B lists the agencies that will supply more specific information. Attention is called, in particular, to *Maine's Coastal Program*, a book published by the State Planning Office that summarizes Maine's Coastal Core Laws.

The Alteration of Coastal Wetlands Act and its rules

The Alteration of Coastal Wetlands Act was enacted by the state legislature in 1969 and has been significantly modified several times by new regulations, most recently in 1987. This law prohibits dredging, filling, or other construction in coastal wetlands without a permit from the Board of Environmental Protection (BEP), the state's "environmental jury." A permit is issued if the proposed activity will not unreasonably interfere with the natural flow of waters or with existing recreation and navigation uses, or cause unreasonable soil erosion or unreasonably harm wildlife and fisheries, or unreasonably lower the quality of any waters. As currently enforced, this law prohibits construction in or over salt marshes or regions with extensive salt-tolerant vegetation. The reason for protecting wetlands is that they serve the public by acting as wildlife habitats while at the same time reducing the impact of coastal floods and enhancing coastal fisheries.

Since passage of the law, serious attempts to site housing developments on marshes have been defeated by the BEP. In one instance in Kittery a mini-mall was ordered to be moved and its builder fined because of illegal siting of the project on a salt marsh.

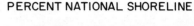

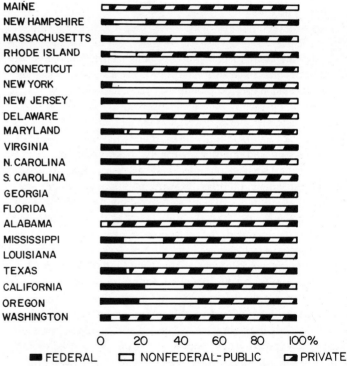

Figure 5.1 Shoreline ownership in the United States. Maine has the greatest amount of privately owned, least publicly accessible coast in the country. (Modified from the National Shoreline Inventory of the U.S. Army Corps of Engineers.)

In mud flat and related intertidal environments water-dependent users such as boat yards and wharves are generally issued construction permits when there are no alternative sites for their activities available. The town of Wiscasset was denied a permit to construct a parking lot on a mud flat, however, since alternative locations existed. The town of Belfast was similarly not permitted to fill a rocky flat to create a beach. In the latter instance the Army Corps of Engineers attempted to circumvent the law by describing the project as "beach erosion control and nourishment."

Following the destructive winter storms that caused $47 million in damage to coastal properties in 1978, the legislature amended the Wetlands Law in 1979 to allow the BEP to better regulate construction in sand dune environments. The regulations generally prevent unreasonable interference with the natural supply or movement of sand within the sand dune system, or unreasonable interference with existing wildlife or recreational uses of the sand dunes. In addition, construction in sand dunes may not unreasonably increase the erosion hazard to the dunes or cause an unreasonable flood hazard to structures built in dunes. Use of the word "unreasonable" has been deemed ambiguous, and in 1983 and again in 1987 the regulations were tightened to prohibit construction of seawalls on the Maine coast. Construction was similarly forbidden in the V (flood hazard) zone seaward of dunes or on frontal dunes themselves. Furthermore, if existing houses or seawalls are 50 percent or more damaged, the regulations require their movement to safer ground and no new construction in the dangerous area. New construction must be proved "safe" from storms or erosion for at least 100 years based on the assumption that sea level will rise 3 feet in the next century.

These regulations have had a generally favorable and immediate impact on coastal development. In one instance on Popham Beach a dwelling constructed on the site of a previously destroyed cottage was denied an after-the-fact permit and ordered removed by the BEP. This decision was upheld by the Maine Supreme Court, which also decided that the state did not owe the cottage owner compensation for loss of property. On Old Orchard Beach the BEP has denied all applications for high-rise condominiums since new rules took effect in 1988. The primary reason for denial has been that the large structures cannot be moved and would be in the surf zone if sea level rises 1–3 feet in the next century. While the new regulations go a long way toward protecting Maine's beaches, it is not clear how the state will respond to the inevitable major storm of the future that causes widespread damage. In one instance through a special amendment to the sand dune law, property owners on Pine Point were permitted to construct a seawall to save their property. While the legislators were careful to craft the amendment to apply only to one unusual location, it is unclear how they will react to the damage of the next 100-year storm.

The rules that govern construction on the coast are becoming increasingly complex, but fortunately they have become easier for the average homeowner to interpret. A booklet describing the rules has recently been updated and improved ("Protecting Your Coastal Wetland" in appendix B). In addition, maps of geological environments and "geohazards" for all of Maine's major sand beaches have been prepared by the Maine Geological Survey. These have been adopted by the BEP as the "best available data" and permit rapid evaluation of the suitability of a specific lot for development (see "Sand Dune Hazard and Geological Environment Maps" in appendix B).

One weakness in the existing regulations has permitted seawalls to be constructed to protect eroding bluffs. While bulkheads and retaining walls are necessary to prevent damage to roads, bridges, and water-dependent businesses on the coast, increasingly they are built to save poorly sited residences. Frequently, a person buys coastal land, puts an expensive house with a septic system on the edge of a bluff, and then clears the bluff of vegetation to improve the view. Predictably, within a year the bluff slumps and the owner begins the expensive process of saving what remains of the property. Since the mud eroded from coastal bluffs is important to adjacent marshes and flats (fig. 2.18), both property owners and the public stand to profit by regulations that require property be set back a safe distance from bluff edges.

Mandatory Shoreline Zoning Act

One of the earliest attempts to control development on the Maine coast was the Mandatory Shoreline Zoning Act of 1971. This law required municipalities to adopt zoning ordinances covering all areas of their jurisdiction "within 250 feet of normal high tide." Three zoning districts generally exist within zoned towns: Re-source Protection Districts, Limited Residential and Recreational Districts, and General Development Districts.

The Resource Protection District is most restrictive and includes marsh and floodplain areas as well as regions of "unstable soils." Generally, residential and commercial development is precluded from these areas by the law. Limited Residential and Recreational Districts (LRRD) include the majority of most coastal areas, and no construction within 75 feet of normal high water is permitted in these areas. The law further states that structures shall not cover more than 20 percent of a lot and that the first floor be elevated at least 2 feet above the highest flood mark within the past 100 years. Sewage disposal within the LRRD must be located at least 100 feet from high tide, and tree cutting within 50 feet of the shore is restricted to cuts no more than 30 feet wide for every 100 feet of coastline. The General Development District includes zones greater than 2 acres devoted to commercial, industrial, or residential development. This last zone is clearly intended to permit urbanized regions the freedom to promote local economic development.

The Shoreline Zoning Act sounds very progressive and was intended to maintain clean water, protect wildlife, save beautiful areas, and permit public access to the coast. These good intentions have not been backed up with adequate enforcement, however, and this is a widely violated state environmental law. Responsibility for the law has recently been passed to the Department of Environmental Protection (DEP), and there is hope that the law will be vigorously enforced. More information on the law is available from the state Shoreland Zoning Coordinator in the DEP in Augusta.

The National Flood Insurance Program

The National Flood Insurance Act of 1968 (P.L. 90-448) as amended by the Flood Disaster Protection Act of 1973 (P.L. 92-234) states that the act is aimed in part to "encourage state and local governments [with jurisdiction over] land which is exposed to flood damage to minimize damage caused by flood losses [and to] guide the development of proposed future construction, where practicable, away from locations which are threatened by flood hazards."

The National Flood Insurance Program (NFIP) was enacted to reduce flood losses through floodplain management, thereby reducing federal disaster relief assistance costs, and to shift at least part of the cost of flood losses to those whose presence on the floodplain caused the loss. The program seeks to hold personal losses to a minimum while also relieving the substantial burden placed on public and private disaster relief agencies by poor siting decisions, inadequate planning, and unsuitable construction activities in floodplain areas.

This program is administered by the Federal Emergency Management Agency (FEMA). The program authorizes the sale of federal flood insurance to property owners in participating communities. This form of insurance is virtually unobtainable in the private insurance market. In return for federal flood insurance,

local governments are required to adopt regulations that comply with minimum federal standards. In other words, communities must make sure that buildings are built well and are located on at least fairly safe sites. Governments implement the flood insurance program through zoning and building codes. Most local governments join the program not only because flood insurance on existing structures is subsidized by the federal government, but because nonparticipation would prevent homeowners in these communities from receiving federal financial assistance for construction in flood hazard areas. This financial assistance includes mortgage loans insured by FHA or guaranteed by VA as well as many forms of disaster assistance.

Before you purchase coastal property in Maine you should ask three questions:

1. Is the community a participant in the National Flood Insurance Program? Your realtor, town manager, or the loan officer at a bank should be able to provide this information.

2. Does the community participate in the emergency phase or in the regular phase of the National Flood Insurance Program? This is important because it affects the amount of flood insurance available for dwellings and contents. If the house was built after the date the community joined the regular program and is not properly constructed, the cost of flood insurance could be prohibitive. Communities that participate in the regular program generally have full-coverage insurance available, while emergency program participants will have a maximum ceiling on insurance coverage. Also, participants in the regular program will have adopted

building codes or other ordinances, while those on the emergency program may not have such codes.

3. How likely is it that your chosen homesite will flood, and to what depth? This information is available in the form of a flood map of the community or county prepared by the Federal Emergency Management Agency. These maps come in two forms, depending on the status of the local community within the National Flood Insurance program. Communities in the regular phase of the National Flood Insurance Program have Flood Insurance Rate Maps (FIRM) that delineate the 100-year flood zone (the area likely to be flooded by a storm that is statistically likely to occur once every 100 years). The area of flooding with fast-moving water (velocity zones, or V zones), as well as the elevation of flooding during the 100-year flood, are shown on the maps. Emergency program communities have Flood Hazard Boundary Maps (FHBM) that delineate only the approximate areas of the 100-year floodplain. If detailed information does not exist in city hall in the form of a FIRM or FHBM, the U.S. Army Corps of Engineers or the Soil Conservation Service may have specific flood information for the property.

Usually the local government will be able to answer any questions about the status of the community within the flood insurance program and the availability of maps or other information. Most lending institutions also will have this information because they are required to inform prospective purchasers of the property's flood hazards prior to the close of sale. Further information is available from the coastal program manager at the State Planning Office in Augusta.

Since October 1981 all residential buildings placed in velocity zones (V zones) must meet elevation requirements higher than the 100-year flood elevation to accommodate potential wave height (usually 3 to 8 feet) and may be charged higher actuarial insurance rates. Nonresidential structures may not have to be elevated but must be "floodproofed" in order to be eligible for insurance. General eligibility requirements vary among pole houses, mobile homes, and condominiums. It is important to note that current regulations under the Sand Dune Law (described above) do not permit new construction in a V zone.

Government literature states that the National Flood Insurance Program would not have been necessary "had adequate and assured flood insurance been available through the private insurance market." The point is that private insurance companies operate on sound business principles. They know that property located in high hazard zones such as floodplains or barrier beaches is a great risk, both physically and financially. For this reason the National Flood Insurance Program was developed to compensate owners in high flood-risk areas. However, as the program grows in experience, it is moving away from subsidized insurance toward a sounder actuarial rate base. Even big government learns economics.

The National Flood Insurance Program has some flaws. Probably the most frequent complaint is that the boundaries of the flood insurance rate maps are inaccurate or difficult to use, but there is an appeal system designed to solve these problems. Another claim is that flood insurance encourages individuals to buy or build homes in disaster areas. Studies of insurance purchasers are mixed on this score, but availability of flood insurance certainly does nothing to discourage construction in high-risk areas. In fact, along the south shore of Massachusetts several homes have been destroyed and rebuilt as many as three times, all with the aid of federal flood insurance.

Perhaps the greatest obstacle to the program's success is the uninformed individual who stands to gain the most from it. One study examined public response to flood insurance and found that many people had little awareness of it or its cost, and they viewed insurance as an investment with the expectation of a return rather than as a means of sharing the cost of natural disasters.

Prospective homeowners should be aware of moves in Congress to alter the structure of the flood insurance program. Already a much greater share of the cost for the program has been shifted away from the taxpayer to the property owner, causing a dramatic rise in premiums. Also, the Coastal Barrier Resource Act enacted by Congress in October 1982 has made any new structures built in certain designated areas after October 1983 ineligible for coverage (see the section on this law later in this chapter). This trend will continue.

Some flood insurance facts

It is important to know the difference between a homeowner's policy and a flood insurance policy.

1. Flood insurance offers the potential flood victim a less expensive and broader form of protection than would be available through a post-disaster loan.

2. Flood insurance is a separate policy from homeowner's insurance. For water damage, for example, the latter covers only structural damage from wind or wind-driven rain.

3. Flood insurance covers losses that result from the general and temporary flooding of normally dry land, the overflow of inland or tidal water, and the unusual and rapid accumulation of surface water runoff from any source.

Check to see if your property location has been identified as flood-prone on the federal Flood Insurance Rate Map (FIRM). As mentioned earlier, if you are located in a flood-prone area you must purchase flood insurance to be eligible for all forms of federal or federally related financial, building, or acquisition assistance —that is, VA and FHA mortgages, SBA loans, and similar programs. To locate your property on the FIRM map, see your insurance agent. Also keep in mind:

1. You need a separate policy for each structure.

2. If you own the building, you can insure structure and contents, or contents only, or structure only.

3. If you rent the building, you need only insure the contents. A separate policy is required to insure the property of each tenant.

For flood insurance purposes, a condominium unit that is a traditional town house or row house is considered as a single-family dwelling, and the individual units may be insured separately. Mobile homes are eligible for coverage if they are on foundations, whether or not permanent, and regardless of whether the wheels are removed either at the time of purchase or while on the foundation.

Structures and items that are not eligible for flood insurance are travel trailers and campers; fences, retaining walls, seawalls, septic tanks, and outdoor swimming pools; gas and liquid storage tanks, wharves, piers, bulkheads, growing crops, shrubbery, land, livestock, roads, or motor vehicles.

Flood insurance policies for residential and commercial properties and/or their contents may be purchased from any licensed property or casualty insurance agent, provided that your community is in the program. One insurance broker cannot charge you more than another for the same flood insurance policy because the federal government subsidizes and sets the rates.

There is normally a five-day waiting period from the date of purchase to the date that coverage becomes effective. The waiting period can be waived at the closing of a mortgage when the community joins the emergency program or converts to the regular program.

Again, if you are buying property located in an *A* or *V* flood hazard zone, be aware that there are significant restrictions on the construction practices permitted in these areas under the Alteration of Coastal Wetlands Act. It is also worth noting that only a seawall distinguishes *V* flood zones from *C*, relatively nonhazardous areas on many developed beaches. In such locations, as the seawalls are damaged by storms, the boundary is likely to move in a landward direction.

Coastal Barrier Resources Act

On 18 October 1982 the U.S. Congress passed the Coastal Barrier Resources Act (P.L. 97-348). This legislation aims to minimize the wasteful spending of federal tax dollars for development-related activities in higher-risk areas on certain barrier islands on the Atlantic and Gulf coasts and to minimize the loss of valuable fish and wildlife habitat resulting from undesirable development of these areas.

Specifically, the legislation designates areas where the federal government no longer will subsidize the costs of bridges, roads, and infrastructures such as sewer and water lines. This legislation does not affect the federal government's involvement in current activities such as maintenance dredging, federal disaster aid, and Coast Guard activities. After October 1, 1983, any new structures built in the designated areas were not eligible for federal flood insurance.

These barriers in Maine falling within the Coastal Barrier system include Seapoint-Crescent beaches, Kittery; Crescent Surf and Parsons beaches, Kennebunk; Scarborough Beach, Scarborough; Main and Strawberry Hill beaches, Cape Elizabeth;

Waldo Point Beach and Jenks Landing Beach, Great Chebeague Island; Head and Hermit Island beaches, Phippsburg; Seven Hundred Acre Island Beach, Isleboro; Popplestone Beach, Jonesport; Starboard Cove and Jasper beaches, Machiasport; Baileys Mistake, West Lubec; Lubec sand and gravel beaches and Carrying Place Heath, Lubec; Birch Point, Eastport; Carrying Place Cove, Harrington; Seal Cove, Cross Island; Bare Cove and Rogue Bluffs, Rogue Bluffs; Flake Point, Jonesport; Over Point, Petit Manan; Pond Island, Cape Rosier; Thrumcap, Mount Desert; Nash Point, Hewett Island; Hunnewell and Small Point beaches, Phippsburg; Stover Point, Harpswell; and Phillips Cove, York Beach.

In 1986 Maine P.L. 794 created a state barrier system that also incorporated all of the above locations. This law prevents the expenditure of state money to develop these undeveloped barriers in a way similar to the federal law.

Other laws and policies

A variety of other state laws, together with those discussed above, make up the Coastal Core Law Authorities recently summarized by the Maine State Planning Office (Maine's Coastal Program, August 1986). These laws often regulate freshwater shorelines (lakes, rivers) as well as marine and include:

The Land Use Regulation Law, which affects islands and coastal property in the unorganized towns;

The Site Law and *Subdivision Law*, wide-ranging laws regulating the manner in which property may be divided and developed;

The Freshwater Wetlands Law, which may affect development on salt marshes that have been altered to freshwater marshes;

The Protection and Improvement of Air Law and *Oil Discharge and Pollution Control Law*, which prevent contamination of coastal air and water mainly by industrial sources;

The Maine Hazardous Waste, Sewage, and Solid Waste Management Act, which prevents untreated sewage and other waste from being introduced into coastal waters;

The Alteration of Rivers, Streams, and Brooks Law, which requires permits from individuals altering freshwater and estuarine shorelines and channels;

The Marine Resources Law, which gives power to the commissioner of the Department of Marine Resources to adopt regulations to promote the conservation and propagation of marine organisms;

The Maine Waterways Development and Conservation Act, which controls construction of dams on tidally influenced streams.

In addition to the laws cited above, in 1986 the legislature passed an *Act to Enhance the Sound Use and Management of Maine's Coastal Resources* (38 MRSA, s. 1801). This act directs public agencies to conduct their activities consistent with the following policies:

1. *Port and harbor development*. Promote the maintenance, development, and revitalization of the state's ports and harbors for fishing, transportation, and recreation.

2. *Marine resources management*. Manage the marine environment and its related resources to preserve and improve the ecological integrity and diversity of marine communities and habitats. Expand our understanding of the productivity of the Gulf of Maine and coastal waters and enhance the economic value of the state's renewable marine resources.

3. *Shoreline management and access*. Support shoreline management that gives preference to water-dependent uses over other uses, that promotes public access to the shoreline, and that considers the cumulative effects of development on coastal resources.

4. *Hazard area development*. Discourage growth and new development in coastal areas where, because of coastal storms, flooding, landslides, or sea level rise, it is hazardous to human health and safety.

5. *State and local cooperative management*. Encourage and support cooperative state and municipal management of coastal resources.

6. *Scenic and natural areas protection*. Protect and manage critical habitat and natural areas of state and national significance and maintain the scenic beauty and character of the coast even in areas where development occurs.

7. *Recreation and tourism*. Expand the opportunities for outdoor recreation and encourage appropriate coastal tourist activities and development.

8. *Water quality*. Restore and maintain the quality of our fresh, marine, and estuarine waters to allow for the broadest possible diversity of public and private uses.

9. *Air quality*. Restore and maintain coastal air quality to protect the health of citizens and visitors and to protect enjoyment of the natural beauty and maritime characteristics of the Maine coast.

These policies may have far-reaching effects if public agencies begin to adopt tougher new regulations affecting the rapid development of Maine's coast.

For more information on specific regulations, necessary permits, and contact agencies, refer to appendix B.

6 Building or buying a house near the beach

In reading this book you may have concluded that the authors seem to be at cross-purposes. On the one hand, we point out that building on the coast is risky. On the other hand, we provide you with a guide to evaluate the risks, and in this chapter we describe how best to buy or build a house near the beach.

This apparent contradiction is more rational than it might seem at first. For those who will heed the warning, we describe the risks of owning shorefront property. But we also realize that coastal development will continue because some individuals will always be willing to gamble their fortunes to be near the shore. For those who elect to play this game of real estate roulette, we provide some advice on improving the odds, on reducing (not eliminating) the risks. We do not recommend, however, that you play the game.

If you want to learn more about construction near the beach, we recommend the book *Coastal Design: A Guide for Builders, Planners, and Homeowners*, which gives more detail on coastal construction and may be used to supplement this volume. In addition, the Federal Emergency Management Agency's *Coastal Construction Manual* is an informative manual for coastal construction that contains much reference material. (See appendix C for a list of publications.)

Coastal realty versus coastal reality

Coastal property is not the same as inland property. Do not approach it as if you were buying a lot in a developed town or a subdivided farm field in an inland area. The previous chapters illustrate that the shores of Maine, especially the barriers, capes, and spits are composed of variable environments and are subjected to nature's most powerful and persistent forces. The reality of the coast is its dynamic character. Property lines are an artificial grid superimposed on this dynamic system. If you choose to place yourself or others in this zone, prudence is in order. A quick glance at the architecture of the structures on the Main coast provides convincing evidence that the reality of coastal processes was rarely considered in their construction.

New construction and major renovation projects must adhere to local building codes and to Federal Insurance Administration (FIA) guidelines. However, many structures along the coastline were built before the adoption of building code and FIA guidelines. Town building officials enforced whatever codes were used; hence, there is a wide disparity in the safety of these structures.

Life's important decisions are based on an evaluation of the facts. Few of us buy goods, choose a career, take legal, financial, or medical actions without first evaluating the facts and seeking advice. In the case of coastal property two general areas should be considered: (1) site safety and (2) the integrity of the structure relative to the forces to which it will be subjected.

Chapter 4 offers a guide to evaluating the site or sites that interest you on the Maine coast. This chapter focuses on the structure itself, whether cottage, condominium, or mobile home.

The structure: concept of balanced risk

The inevitability of a structure's eventual destruction becomes obvious when one considers the inescapable influences of time, environment, and economic factors. The objective of good building design therefore is to create a structure that is both economically feasible and functionally reliable; a house must be affordable and have a reasonable life expectancy. To create such a house, a balance must be achieved among financial, structural, and environmental considerations. Most of these considerations are heightened on the coast—property values are higher, the environment is more sensitive, and the likelihood of storms and other hazards is greater.

The individual who builds or buys a home in an exposed area should fully comprehend the risks involved and the chance of harm to home or family. The risks should then be weighed against the benefits to be derived from living there. Similarly, the developer who is putting up a motel should weigh the possibility of destruction and death during a major storm against economic advantages to be gained from such a building. Then and only then should construction proceed. For both the homeowner and the developer, proper construction and location reduce the risks involved.

The concept of balanced risk should take into account the following fundamental considerations:

1. A coastal structure is exposed to high winds, waves, or flooding and should be stronger than a structure built inland.

2. A building with high occupancy, such as an apartment building, should be safer than a building with low occupancy, such as a single-family dwelling.

3. A building that houses elderly or sick people should be safer than a building housing able-bodied people.

4. Because construction must be economically feasible, ultimate and total safety is not obtainable for most homeowners on the coast.

5. A building with a planned long life, such as a year-round residence, should be stronger than a building with a planned short life, such as a mobile home or a summer cottage.

Structures can be designed and built within reasonable economic limits to resist all but the largest storms. Structural engineering is the designing and constructing of buildings to withstand the forces of nature. It is based on a knowledge of the forces to which the structures will be subjected and an understanding of the strength of building materials. The effectiveness of structural engineering design is reflected in the statistics of typhoon Tracy, which struck Darwin, Australia in 1974. Seventy percent of housing that was not based on structural engineering principles was destroyed and 20 percent was seriously damaged—only 10 percent of the housing weathered the storm. In contrast, over 70 percent of the structurally engineered large commercial, government, and industrial buildings came through with little or no damage, and less than 5 percent of such structures were destroyed. Because housing accounts for more than half of the capital cost of the buildings in Queensland, the state government established a building code that requires standardized structural engineering for houses in hurricane-prone areas. This improvement has been achieved with little increase in construction and design costs.

Coastal forces: design requirements

Hurricanes and major storms, with their associated high winds and storm surge topped by large waves, are the most destructive of the forces to be reckoned with on the coast. However, in Maine the frequency of hurricanes is much less than that of northeasters. It is the northeasters that bring the greater amount of damage. (Figure 6.1 illustrates the effects of hurricane and storm forces on houses and other structures.)

Winds can be evaluated in terms of the pressure they exert. The pressure varies with the square of the velocity, the height above the ground, and the shape of the object against which the wind is blowing. For example, a 100-mph wind exerts a pressure or force of about 40 pounds per square foot (psf) on a flat surface such as a sign. The pressure the same wind exerts on a curved surface such as a sphere or cylinder is much less—about half that of the flat surface. If the wind picks up to a velocity of 190 mph, the force increases to 140 psf on the flat surface.

Wind velocity increases with height above ground, so a tall structure is subject to greater velocity and thereby greater pressure than a low structure. The velocity and corresponding pressure could be almost double at 100 feet above the ground than that at ground level. Because the wind pressure increases with the height above ground of an object and is modified by the shape of the object, pressure on an outdoor sign or a high chimney will be greater than on a low octagonal or round object.

A house or building designed for inland areas is built primarily to resist vertical loads. It is assumed that the foundation and framing must support the load of the walls, floor, roof, furniture, and relatively insignificant wind forces.

A well-built house in a hurricane- or storm-prone area, however, must be constructed to withstand a variety of strong wind forces that may come from any direction. Although many people think that wind damage is caused by uniform horizontal pressures (lateral loads), most damage, in fact, is caused by uplift (vertical), suctional (pressure outward from within the house), and twisting (torsional) forces. High horizontal pressure on the windward side is accompanied by suction on the leeward side. The roof is subject both to downward pressure and, more importantly, to uplift. Often a roof is sucked up by the uplift drag of the wind. Usually the failure of houses is in the devices that connect the parts of the structure together. All structural members (beams, rafters, columns) should be fastened together on the assumption that about 25 percent of the vertical load on the member may be a force coming from any direction (sideways or upward). Such structural integrity is also important if it is possible the structure may have to be moved to avoid destruction by shoreline retreat.

WIND

Arrows show direction of
forces on house.

WAVES

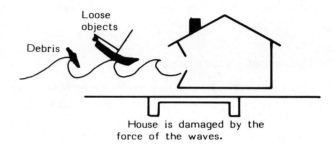

House is damaged by the
force of the waves.

DROP IN BAROMETRIC PRESSURE

The passing eye of the storm
creates different pressure inside
and out, and high pressure inside
attempts to burst house open.

HIGH WATER

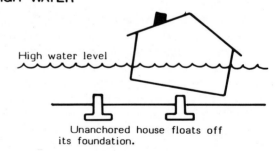

Unanchored house floats off
its foundation.

Figure 6.1. Forces to be reckoned with at the shoreline.

Storm surge

Storm surge is the rise above normal sea level during a storm. During hurricanes and storms, the coastal zone is inundated by storm surge and accompanying storm waves, and these cause most property damage and loss of life.

Often the pressure of the wind backs water into streams or estuaries already swollen from the exceptional rainfall brought on by the storm. This flooding is particularly dangerous when the wind pressure keeps the tide from running out of inlets, so that the next normal high tide pushes the accumulated waters back still higher. Flooding can cause an unanchored house to float off its foundation and come to rest against another house, severely damaging both.

Disaster preparedness officials have pointed out that it is a sad fact that even many condominiums built on pilings are not anchored or tied to those pilings, just set on top of them. Even if the house itself is left structurally intact, flooding may destroy its contents. People who have cleaned the mud and contents out of a house subjected to flooding retain vivid memories of its effects.

Proper coastal development takes into account the expected level and frequency of storm surge for the area. In general, building standards require that the first habitable floor of a dwelling be above the 100-year flood level plus an allowance for wave height. At this level, a building has a 1 percent probability of being flooded in any given year.

Storm waves

Storm waves can cause severe damage not only by forcing water onshore to flood buildings but also by throwing boats, barges, piers, houses, and other floating debris inland against standing structures. The force of a wave may be understood when one considers that a cubic yard of water weighs over three-fourths of a ton; hence, a breaking wave moving shoreward at a speed of several tens of miles per hour can be one of the most destructive elements of a storm. Waves can also destroy coastal structures by scouring away the underlying sand, causing them to collapse. It is possible to design buildings to survive crashing storm surf; many lighthouses, for example, have survived numerous storms. But in the balanced risk equation, it usually is not economically feasible to build ordinary cottages to resist the more powerful of such forces. On the other hand, cottages can be made considerably more storm-worthy by following the suggestions in the rest of this chapter.

Battering by debris

Even though it may be an isolated occurrence, the likelihood of a floating object of a normally encountered size striking a house should be taken into account. To get an idea of the size of a battering load which the house should be designed to protect against, we go to the Model Minimum Hurricane Resistant Building Standards for the Texas Gulf Coast, which specifies: "The normal battering

load shall be considered as a concentrated load acting horizon-
tally at the [100-year flood level plus wave height] or at any point
below it, equal to the impact force produced by a 1,000 pound
mass travelling at a velocity of 10 feet per second and acting on
a one-square-foot surface of the structure."

For certain buildings such as "safe refuges," the above standards
specify that they be constructed to resist battering loads more
severe than normal ones. This refers to a building or structure
located in the flood area with space sufficiently above the high
water level to be authorized as a safe refuge or haven in the event
of a hurricane.

Barometric pressure change

Changes in barometric pressure may also be a minor contributor to
structural failure. If a house is sealed at a normal barometric pressure of 30 inches of mercury, and the external pressure suddenly
drops to 26.61 inches of mercury (as it did in Hurricane Camille in
Mississippi in 1969), the pressure exerted within the house would
be 245 pounds per square foot. An ordinary house would explode
if it were leakproof. In tornadoes, where there is a severe pressure
differential, many houses do burst. In hurricanes and storms the
problem is much less severe. Fortunately, most houses leak, but
they must leak fast enough to prevent damage. Many people seal
up cracks in their houses to save energy. This has some bad as
well as good results. Leaks are reduced, but so is venting capac-
ity. Also the quality of inside air may deteriorate more than is

desirable, especially with certain types of heaters. Venting the
underside of the roof at the eaves is a common means of equalizing
internal and external pressure. Given the more destructive forces of
storm winds and waves, however, pressure differentials may be
a minor concern. Figure 6.2 illustrates some of the actions that a
homeowner can take to deal with the forces just described.

House selection

Some types of houses are more suited for the shore than others,
and an awareness of the differences will help you make a better
selection, whether you are building a new house or buying an
existing one.

Worst of all are unreinforced masonry houses, whether brick,
concrete block, hollow clay tile, or brick veneer because they cannot withstand the lateral forces of wind and wave, the battering by
debris, the flooding, the scour and the settling of the foundation.
Adequate and extraordinary reinforcing will alleviate the inherent
weakness of unit masonry, if done properly. Reinforced concrete
and steel frames are excellent but are rarely used in the construction of small residential structures.

It is hard to beat a wood frame house that is properly braced
and anchored and has well-connected members. The well-built
wood house will often hold together as a unit, even if moved off
its foundations, when other types disintegrate. It is also the easiest
to move back or raise to a safer level. In addition to the above, the
building must be designed (or modified) and adequately anchored

Problem:
Higher pressure inside than out.

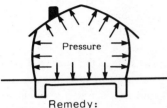

Pressure

Remedy:
Open windows on lee side of the
house. Put vents in the attic to
equalize the pressure.

Problem:
Overturning and lateral movement

Wind or
waves

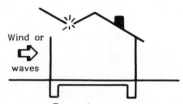

Remedy:
Anchor house to foundation with
tension connection.

Problem:
Loss of parts of house.

Wind or
waves

Remedy:
Install adequate connections and
properly sized materials.

Problem:
Racking (lateral collapse).

Wind or
waves

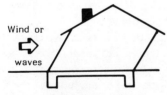

Remedy:
Install bracing, such as diagonals
and plywood sheets well nailed to
studs and floor plates; in masonry
houses, install reinforcing.

Problem:
Penetration by flying debris.

Flying
debris

Wind or
waves

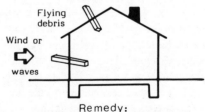

Remedy:
Construct walls and roof solidly.
Make windows extra strong; use
smaller panes.

Figure 6.2. Modes of failure and how to deal with them. (Modified
from U.S. Civil Defense Preparedness Agency Publication TR-83.)

to prevent flotation collapse, or lateral movement. It must be constructed with materials and utility equipment resistant to flood damage.

Keeping dry: building on the sand—pole or stilt houses

In coastal regions subject to flooding by waves or storm surge, the best and most common method of minimizing damage is to raise the lowest floor of a residence above the expected level. Also, the first habitable floor of a home must be above the 100-year storm surge level (plus calculated wave height) to qualify for federal flood insurance.

Nonresidential buildings should also be floodproofed at least up to the base flood level and/or elevated at or above this level. Where the soil is suitable, most modern flood zone structures should be constructed on piling, well anchored in the subsoils. Elevating the structure by building a mound is generally not suited to the coastal zone because mounded soil is easily eroded.

Current building design criteria for pole house construction under the flood insurance program are outlined in the book *Elevated Residential Structures* (Appendix C). Regardless of insurance, pole-type construction with deeply embedded poles is best in areas where waves and storm surge will erode foundation material. Materials used in pole construction include the following:

Piles are long, slender columns of wood, steel, or concrete driven into the earth to a sufficient depth to support the vertical load of the house and to withstand horizontal forces of flowing water, wind, and waterborne debris. Pile construction is especially suitable in areas where scouring (soil washing out from under the foundation of a house) is a problem.

Posts are usually posts of wood; if made of steel, they are called columns. Unlike piles, they are not driven into the ground, but, rather, are placed in a pre-dug hole at the bottom of which may be a concrete pad (fig. 6.3). Posts may be held in place by backfilling and tamping earth, or by pouring concrete into the hole after the post is in place. Posts are more readily aligned than driven piles and are, therefore, better to use if poles must extend to the roof. In general, treated wood is the cheapest and most common material for both posts and piles.

Piers are vertical supports, thicker than piles or posts, usually made of reinforced concrete or reinforced masonry (concrete blocks or bricks). They are set on footings and extend to the underside of the floor frame.

Pole construction can be of two types. The poles can be cut off at the first-floor level to support the platform that serves as the dwelling floor. In this case, piles, posts, or piers can be used. Or they can be extended to the roof and rigidly tied into both the floor and the roof. In this way they become major framing members for the structure and provide better anchorage to the house as a whole (figs. 6.4, 6.5). A combination of full and floor height poles is used in some cases, with the shorter poles restricted to supporting the floor inside the house (fig. 6.6).

Where the foundation material can be eroded by waves or

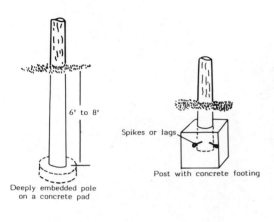

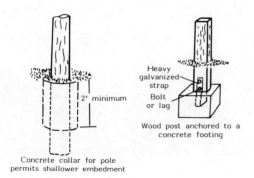

Figure 6.3. Shallow and deep supports for poles and posts. Source: Southern Pine Association.

winds, the poles should be deeply embedded and solidly anchored either by driving piles or by drilling deep holes for posts and putting in a concrete pad at the bottom of each hole. Where the embedment is shallow, a concrete collar around the poles improves anchorage (fig. 6.3). The choice depends on the soil conditions. Piles are more difficult than posts to align to match the house frame. Posts can be positioned in the holes before backfilling. In either case, the foundations must be deep enough to provide support after maximum predicted loss of sand from storm erosion and scour. This required depth will often dictate piles rather than posts.

Piles have the advantage of permitting far better penetration at a reasonable cost. Insufficient depth of pile or post will cause failure if storm waves liquify and erode the sand support. Improper connections of floor to piling and inadequate pile bracing will contribute to structural failure. Just as important as driving the pilings deep enough to resist scouring and to support the loads they must carry is the need to fasten them securely to the structure above them which they support. The connections must resist both horizontal loads and uplift from wind and waves during a storm.

When post holes are dug, rather than pilings driven, the posts should extend 4 to 8 feet into the ground to provide anchorage. The lower end of the post should rest on a concrete pad, spreading the load to the soil over a greater area to prevent settlement. Where the soil is sandy or is the type that the embedment can be less than 6 feet, it is best to tie the post down to the footing with straps or other anchoring devices to prevent uplift. Driven piles should have a minimum penetration of 8 feet. However, most soils require

Figure 6.4. Pole house, with poles extending to the roof. Extending poles to the roof, as shown in this photograph, instead of the usual method of cutting them off at the first floor, strengthens a beach cottage. Photo by Orrin H. Pilkey, Jr.

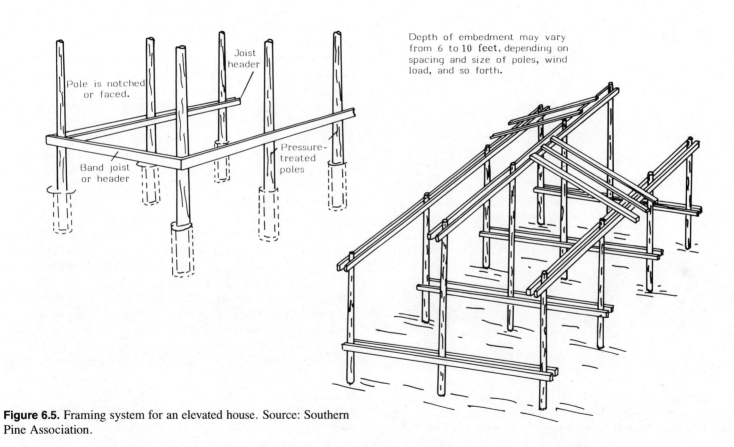

Pole is notched
or faced.

Joist
header

Band joist
or header

Pressure-
treated
poles

Depth of embedment may vary
from 6 to 10 feet, depending on
spacing and size of poles, wind
load, and so forth.

Figure 6.5. Framing system for an elevated house. Source: Southern
Pine Association.

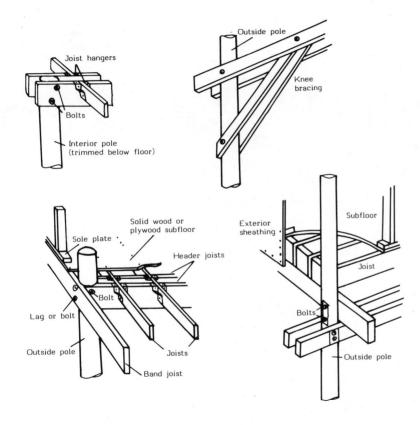

Figure 6.6. Tying floors to poles. Source: Southern Pine Association.

greater embedment, and code requirements for specific situations may determine the level. If the site is near the water, greater embedment is needed.

As mentioned above, it is important to embed piles well below the depth of potential scour. Some localities require that the piles be driven to a depth of at least 10 feet below mean sea level. The floor and the roof should be securely connected to the poles with bolts or other fasteners. When the floor rests on poles that do not extend to the roof, attachment is even more critical. A system of metal straps is often used. Unfortunately, builders sometimes inadequately attach the girders, beams, and joists to the supporting poles with too few and undersized bolts. Hurricanes have proven this to be insufficient.

Local building codes may specify the size, quality, and spacing of the piles, ties, and bracing, as well as the methods of fastening the structure to them. Building codes often are minimal requirements, however, and building inspectors are usually willing to allow designs that are equally or more effective.

The space under an elevated house, regardless of construction type, must be kept free of obstructions in order to minimize the impact of waves and floating debris. If the space is enclosed, the enclosing walls should be designed so that they can break away or fall under flood loads. The enclosing walls should be designed to either remain attached to the house or be heavy enough to sink. Thus the walls cannot float away and add to the waterborne debris problem. Alternative ways of avoiding this problem are designing walls that can be swung up out of the path of the floodwaters, or building them with louvers that allow the water to pass through. The louvered wall is subject to damage from floating debris. The convenience of closing in the ground floor for a garage, storage, or recreation room may be costly because it may violate insurance requirements and actually contribute to the loss of the house in a hurricane. The design of the enclosing breakaway walls should be checked against insurance requirements. (See *Elevated Residential Structures*, Appendix C.)

Building on rocks

Many words have been written about how to build structures that can best resist storms, hurricanes, and floods. But no better advice can be given than that contained in Matthew 7:24–47 and Luke 6:47–49: "a wise man . . . built his house upon a rock and the rain descended and the floods came, and the winds blew, and beat upon the house; and it fell not for it was founded upon a rock" and "a foolish man . . . built his house upon the sand and the rain descended and the floods came, and the winds blew, and beat upon the house; and it fell and great was the fall thereof."

We are lucky along parts of the Maine coast to have rocks on which to build our houses. In the following paragraphs we hope to advise you on how best to build on the rocks along our coast. One of the most critical aspects of building in a coastal area is the method of anchoring to the ground, whether it be sand or rock, and of connecting the structural members from foundation to rooftop. Building on rock presents its own problems.

Although scouring and erosion may not be as severe as on sandy soil, high winds, flooding, and battering by debris are still destructive forces. Anchoring of the house to the ground is absolutely essential. This can be accomplished by one of several means:

A hole can be drilled in the rock and filled with quick-set mortar into which a bar is driven. The upper end of the bar is threaded and is equipped with a nut and washer for fastening to the floor system.

Another method is to drill a hole in the rock and widen the bottom to a greater diameter than the top. Then insert a bar with a plate or washer on its lower end and grout. As above, the upper end is threaded and equipped with nut and washer.

Rock bolts are available with expansion head assemblies. This gives a single point contact between the steel bar and the rock wall, which can be supplemented with grout. Epoxy or resin grout as well as cement grout can be used with these rock bolts or rock anchors.

The bolts described above resist uplift; to be effective they must be securely fastened to the floor system of the house. More conventional supports must, of course, be provided to support loads imposed by gravity, that is, the weight of the building, plus the objects and people therein.

An existing house: what to look for

If instead of building a new house, you are selecting a house already built in an area subject to flooding and high winds, consider the following factors: (1) where the house is located, (2) how well the house is built, and (3) how the house can be improved.

Geographic location

Evaluate the site of an existing house using the same principles given earlier for evaluating a possible site to build a new house. House elevation, frequency of high water, escape route, and how well the lot drains should be emphasized, but you should also go through the complete site safety checklist.

You can modify the house after you have purchased it, but you cannot prevent hurricanes or other storms. The first step is to stop and consider: do the pleasures and benefits of this location balance the risks and disadvantages? If not, look elsewhere for a home; if so, then evaluate the house itself.

How well built is the house?

In general, the principles used to evaluate an existing house are the same as those used in building a new one. It should be remembered that many of the houses were built prior to the enactment of the National Flood Insurance Program and may not meet the standards required of structures or improvements built since then.

Before you thoroughly inspect the building in which you are interested, look closely at the adjacent structures. If poorly built, they may float over against your building and damage it in a flood. You may even want to consider the type of people you will have as neighbors; will they "clear the decks" in preparation for a storm or will they leave items in the yard to become wind-borne missiles?

The house or condominium itself should be inspected for the following:

The structure should be well anchored to the ground. If it is simply resting on blocks, rising water may cause it to float off its foundation and come to rest against your neighbor's house or out in the middle of the street. If well built and well braced internally, it may be possible to move the house back to its proper location, but chances are great that the house will be too damaged to be habitable.

If the building is on piles, posts, or poles, check to see if the floor beams are adequately bolted to them. If it rests on piers, crawl under the house if space permits to see if the floor beams are securely connected to the foundation. If the floor system rests unanchored on piers, do not buy the house.

It is difficult to discern whether a structure built on a concrete slab is properly bolted to the slab because the inside and outside walls hide the bolts. If you can locate the builder, ask if such bolting was done. Better yet, if you can get assurance that construction of the house complied with the provisions of a building code serving the needs of that particular region, you can be reasonably sure that all parts of the house are well anchored. Be sure to check the anchorage of the foundation to the ground, the floor to the foundation, the walls to the floor, and the roof to the walls (figs. 6.7, 6.8, 6.9). Be aware that many builders, carpenters, and building inspectors who are accustomed to traditional construc-

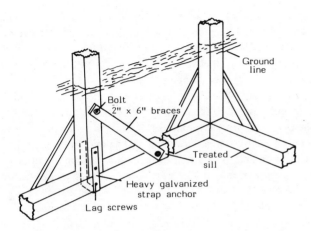

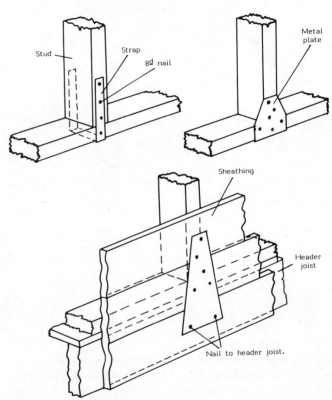

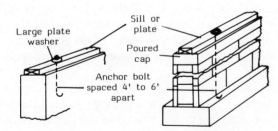

Figure 6.7. Foundation anchorage. Top: anchored sill for shallow embedment. Bottom: anchoring sill or plate to foundation. Source of bottom drawing: *Houses Can Resist Hurricanes*, U.S. Forest Service Research Paper FPL 33.

Figure 6.8. Stud-to-floor, plate-to-floor framing methods. Source: *Houses Can Resist Hurricanes*, U.S. Forest Service Research Paper FPL 33.

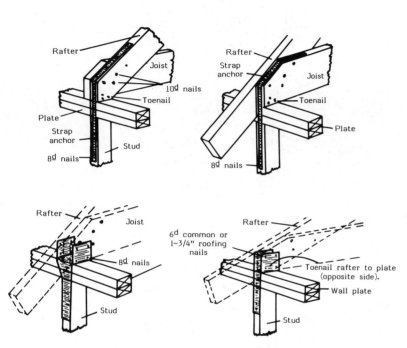

Figure 6.9. Roof-to-wall connectors. The top drawings show metal strap connectors: left, rafter to stud; right, joist to stud. The bottom left drawing shows a double-member metal plate connector—in this case with the joist to the right of the rafter. The bottom right drawing shows a single-member metal plate connector. Source: *Houses Can Resist Hurricanes*, U.S. Forest Service Research Paper FPL 33.

tion are apt to regard metal connectors, collar beams, and other such devices as newfangled and unnecessary. If consulted, they may assure you that a house is as solid as a rock, when, in fact, it is far from it. Nevertheless, it is wise to consult the builder or knowledgeable neighbors when possible.

The roof should be well anchored to the walls. This will prevent uplifting and separation from the walls. Visit the attic to see if such anchoring exists. Simple toenailing (nailing at an angle) is not adequate—metal fasteners are needed. Depending on the type of construction and the amount of insulation laid on the floor of the attic, these may or may not be easy to see. If roof trusses or braced rafters were used, it should be easy to see whether the various members, such as the diagonals, are well fastened together. Again, simple toenailing will not suffice. Some builders, unfortunately, nail parts of a roof truss just enough to hold it together to get it in place. A collar beam or gusset at the peak of the roof (fig. 6.10) provides some assurance of good construction. The Standard Building Code states that wood truss rafters shall be securely fastened to the exterior walls with approved hurricane anchors or clips.

Quality roofing material should be well anchored to the sheathing. A poor roof covering will be destroyed by hurricane-force winds, allowing rain to enter the house and damage ceilings, walls, and the contents of the house. Galvanized nails (two per shingle) should be used to connect wood shingles and shakes to wood sheathing and should be long enough to penetrate through the sheathing (fig. 6.10). Threaded nails should be used for plywood

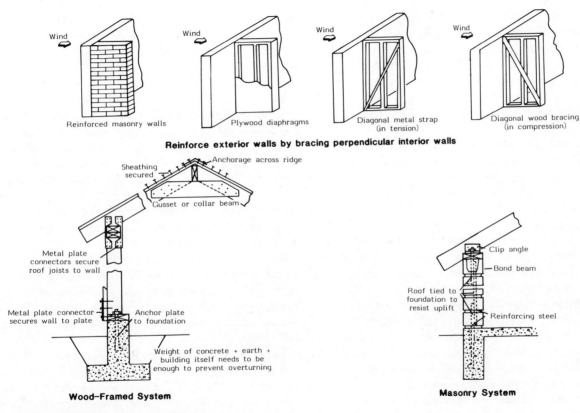

Wind

Reinforced masonry walls

Wind

Plywood diaphragms

Wind

Diagonal metal strap
(in tension)

Wind

Diagonal wood bracing
(in compression)

Reinforce exterior walls by bracing perpendicular interior walls

Sheathing
secured

Anchorage across ridge

Gusset or collar beam

Metal plate
connectors secure
roof joists to wall

Metal plate connector
secures wall to plate

Anchor plate
to foundation

Weight of concrete + earth +
building itself needs to be
enough to prevent overturning

Wood-Framed System

Clip angle

Bond beam

Roof tied to
foundation to
resist uplift

Reinforcing steel

Masonry System

Figure 6.10. Where to strengthen a house. (Modified from U.S. Civil Defense Preparedness Agency Publication TR-83.)

sheathing. Sheathing is the covering (usually woodboards, plywood, or wallboards) placed over rafters, or exterior studding of a building to provide a base for the application of roof or wall cladding. For roof slopes that rise 1 foot for every 3 feet or more of horizontal distance, exposure of the shingle should be about one-fourth of its length (4 inches for a 16-inch shingle). If shakes (thicker and longer than shingles) are used, less than one-third of their length should be exposed.

In hurricane areas, asphalt shingles should be exposed somewhat less than usual. A mastic or seal-tab type, or an interlocking shingle of heavy grade should be used along with a roof underlay of asphalt-saturated felt and galvanized roofing nails or approved staples (6 for each 3-tab strip).

The fundamental rule to remember in framing is that all structural elements should be fastened together and anchored to the ground in such a manner as to resist all forces, regardless of which direction these forces may come from. This prevents overturning, floating off, racking, or disintegration.

The shape of the house is important. A hip roof, which slopes in four directions, is better able to resist high winds than a gable roof, which slopes in two directions. This was found to be true in Hurricane Camille in 1969 in Mississippi and, later in Typhoon Tracy, which devastated Darwin, Australia, in December 1974. The reason is twofold: the hip roof offers a smaller shape for the wind to blow against, and its structure is such that it is better braced in all directions.

Note also the horizontal cross section of the house (the shape of the house as viewed from above). The pressure exerted by a wind on a round or elliptical shape is about 60 percent of that exerted on the common square or rectangular shape. The pressure exerted on a hexagonal or octagonal cross section is about 80 percent of that exerted on a square or rectangular cross section.

The design of a house or building in a coastal area should minimize structural discontinuities and irregularities. It should be plain and simple and have a minimum of nooks and crannies and offsets on the exterior, because damage to a structure tends to concentrate at these points. Some of the newer beach cottages are of a highly angular design with such nooks and crannies. Award-winning architecture will be a storm loser if the design has not incorporated the technology for maximizing structural integrity with respect to storm forces. When irregularities are absent, the house reacts to storm winds as a complete unit.

Brick, concrete block, and masonry wall houses should be adequately reinforced. This reinforcement is hidden from view. Building codes applicable to high wind areas often specify the type of mortar, reinforcing, and anchoring to be used in construction. If you can get assurance that the house was built in compliance with a building code designed for such an area, consider buying it. At all costs, avoid unreinforced masonry houses.

A poured-concrete bond beam at the top of the wall just under the roof is one indication that the house is well built (fig. 6.11). Most bond beams are formed by putting in reinforcing and pouring concrete in U-shaped concrete blocks. From the outside, however, you cannot distinguish these U-shaped blocks from ordinary ones

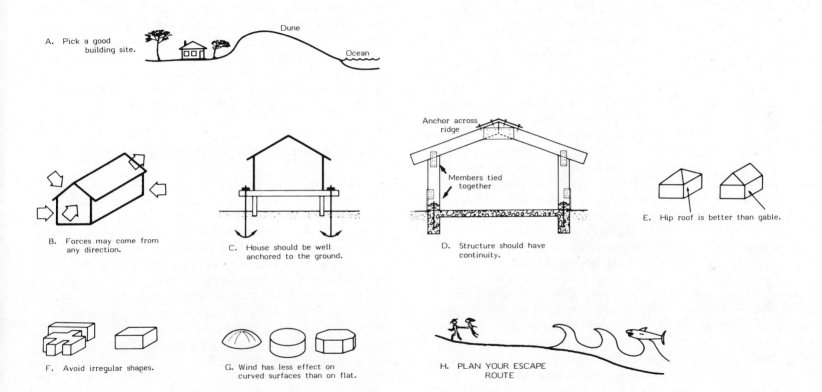

Figure 6.11. Some rules in selecting or designing a house.

and therefore cannot be certain that a bond beam exists. The vertical reinforcing should penetrate the bond beam.

Some architects and builders use a stacked bond (one block directly above another), rather than overlapped or staggered blocks, because they believe it looks better. The stacked bond is definitely weaker than the overlapped. Unless you have proof that the walls are adequately reinforced to overcome this lack of strength, you should avoid this type of construction.

In past hurricanes the brick veneer of many houses has separated from the wood frame, even when the houses remained standing. This type of construction should be avoided along the coast.

Ocean-facing glazing (windows, glass doors, glass panels) should be minimal. Although large open glass areas facing the ocean provide an excellent sea view, such glazing may present several problems. The obvious hazard is glass shattering and blowing inward during a storm. Glass projectiles are lethal. Less frequently recognized problems include the fact that glass may not provide as much structural strength as wood, metal, or other building materials. Ocean-facing glass is commonly damaged through sediment sand blasting, transported by normal coastal winds. The solution to this latter problem may be in reducing the amount of glass in the original design, or installing storm shutters, which come in a variety of materials from steel to wood.

Consult a good architect or structural engineer for advice if you are in doubt about any aspects of a house. A few dollars spent for wise counsel may save you from later financial grief.

To summarize, a beach house should have (1) roof tied to walls, walls tied to foundation, and foundation anchored to the earth (the connections are potentially the weakest link in the structural system); (2) a shape that resists storm forces; (3) floors high enough to be above most storm waters (usually the 100-year flood level plus 3 to 8 feet); (4) piles or posts that are of sufficient depth or embedded in concrete to anchor the structure and to withstand erosion (scour); and (5) piling that is well braced.

What can be done to improve an existing house?

If you presently own a house or are contemplating buying one in a hurricane- or storm-prone area, you will want to know how to improve occupant protection in the house. If so, you should obtain the excellent publication *Wind Resistant Design Concepts for Residences* (appendix C). Of particular interest are the sections on building a refuge shelter module within a residence. Also noteworthy are two supplements to this publication (next entry, appendix C) which deal with buildings larger than single-family residences in urban areas. These provide a means of checking whether the responsible authorities are doing their jobs to protect schools, office buildings, and apartments. Many other pertinent references are listed in appendix C.

Suppose your house is resting on blocks but not fastened to them and, thus, is not adequately anchored to the ground. Can anything be done? One solution is to treat the house like a mobile home by screwing ground anchors into the earth to a depth of 4 feet or more and fastening them to the underside of the floor systems. See figures 6.12 and 6.13 for illustrations of how ground anchors can be used. Methods of anchoring houses built on rock are treated earlier in this chapter.

Calculations to determine the needed number of ground anchors will differ between a house and a mobile home because each is affected differently by the forces of wind and water. Recent practice is to put commercial steel rod anchors in at an angle in order to better align them with the direction of the pull. If a vertical anchor is used, the top 18 inches or so should be encased in a concrete cylinder about 12 inches in diameter. This prevents the top of the anchor rod from bending or slicing through the wet soil from the horizontal component of the pull.

Diagonal struts, either timber or pipe, may also be used to anchor a house that rests on blocks. This is done by fastening the upper ends of the struts to the floor system and by fastening the lower ends to individual concrete footings substantially below the surface of the ground. These struts must be able to withstand both the tension of uplift and the compression of structural weight. The struts should be tied into the concrete footing with anchoring devices such as straps or spikes.

If the house has a porch with exposed columns or posts, it should be possible to install tie-down anchors on their tops and bottoms. Steel straps should suffice in most cases. When accessible, roof rafters and trusses should be anchored to the wall system. Usually the roof trusses or braced rafters are sufficiently exposed to make it possible to strengthen joints (where two or more mem-

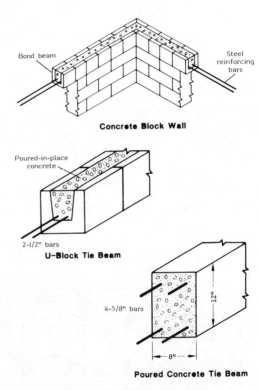

Figure 6.12. Reinforced tie beam (bond beam) for concrete block walls—to be used at each floor level and at roof level around the perimeter of the exterior walls.

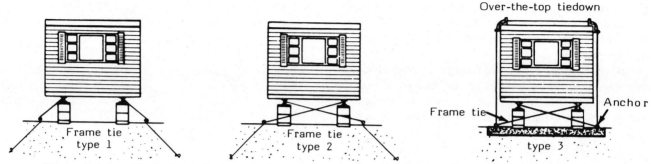

These sketches illustrate various methods for connecting frame ties to the mobile home frame. Type 2 system can resist greater horizontal forces than type 1. Type 3 system involves placement of mobile home on concrete slab. Anchors embedded in concrete slab are connected to ties.

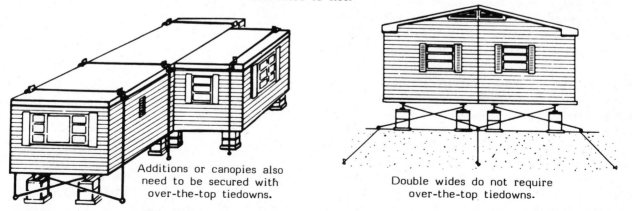

Additions or canopies also need to be secured with over-the-top tiedowns.

Double wides do not require over-the-top tiedowns.

bers meet) with collar beams or gussets, particularly at the peak of the roof (fig. 6.10).

A competent carpenter, architect, or structural engineer can review the house with you and help you decide what modifications are most practical and effective. Do not be misled by someone who is resistant to new ideas. One builder told a homeowner, "You don't want all those newfangled straps and anchoring devices. If you use them, the whole house will blow away, but if you build in the usual manner (with members lightly connected), you may lose only part of it." In fact, the very purpose of the straps is to prevent any or all of the house from blowing away. The Standard Building Code says, "Lateral support securely anchored to all walls provides the best and only sound structural stability against horizontal thrusts, such as winds of exceptional velocity." And the cost of connecting all elements securely adds very little to the cost of the frame of the dwelling, usually under 10 percent, and a very much smaller percentage of the total cost of the house.

If the house has an overhanging eave and there are no openings on its underside, it may be feasible to cut openings and screen them. These openings keep the attic cooler (a plus in the summer) and help to equalize the pressure inside and outside the house during a storm with a low pressure center.

Another way a house can be improved is to modify one room so that it can be used as an emergency refuge in case you are trapped in a major storm. (This is *not* an alternative to evacuation prior to a hurricane or severe northeaster.) Examine the house and select the best room to stay in during a storm. A small windowless room such as a bathroom, utility room, or storage space is usually stronger than a room with windows. A sturdy inner room, with more than one wall between it and the outside, is safest. The fewer doors there are, the better; an adjoining wall or baffle wall shielding the door adds to the protection.

Consider bracing or strengthening the interior walls. Such reinforcement may require removing the surface covering and installing plywood sheathing or strap bracing. Where wall studs are exposed, bracing straps offer a simple way to achieve needed reinforcement against the wind. These straps are commercially produced and are made of 16-gauge galvanized metal with prepunched holes for nailing. These should be secured to studs and wall plates as nail holes permit (fig. 6.10). Bear in mind that they are good only for tension.

If, after reading this, you agree that something should be done to your house, do it now. Do not put it off until the next severe storm hits you!

Mobile homes: limiting their mobility

Because of their light weight and flat sides, mobile homes are vulnerable to the high winds of hurricanes, tornadoes, and severe storms. Such winds can overturn unanchored mobile homes or smash them into neighboring homes and property. Nearly 6 million

Figure 6.13. Tiedowns for mobile homes. Source: U.S. Civil Defense Preparedness Agency Publication TR-75.

Americans live in mobile homes today, and the number is growing. Twenty to 30 percent of single-family housing production in the United States is of mobile homes. High winds damage or destroy nearly 5,000 of these homes every year, and the number will surely rise unless protective measures are taken. As one man whose mobile home was overturned in Hurricane Frederic (1979) so aptly put it, "People who live in flimsy houses shouldn't have hurricanes."

Several lessons can be learned from past experiences in storms. First, mobile homes should be located properly. After Hurricane Camille (1969) it was observed that where mobile home parks were surrounded by woods and where the units were close together, damage was minimized and was caused mainly by falling trees. In unprotected areas, however, many mobile homes were overturned and destroyed from the force of the wind. The protection afforded by a large stand of trees is greater than a single row, and trees 30 feet or more in height give better protection than shorter ones. If possible, position the mobile home so that the narrow side faces the prevailing winds.

Locating a mobile home in a hilltop park will greatly increase its vulnerability to the wind. A lower site screened by trees is safer from the wind, but it should be above storm surge flood levels. A location that is too low obviously increases the likelihood of flooding. There are fewer safe locations for mobile homes than for stilt houses.

A second lesson taught by past experience is that the mobile home must be tied down or anchored to the ground so that it will not overturn in high winds (figs. 6.13, 6.14, and table 6.1). Simple prudence dictates the use of tiedowns. Many insurance companies, moreover, will not insure mobile homes unless they are adequately anchored with tiedowns. A mobile home may be tied down with cable or rope, or rigidly attached to the ground by connecting it to a simple wood post foundation system. An alert mobile home park owner can provide permanent concrete anchors or piers to which hold-down ties may be fastened. In general, an entire tie-down system costs only a nominal amount.

A mobile home should be properly anchored with both ties to the frame and straps over the top; otherwise it may be damaged by sliding, overturning, or tossing. The most common cause of major damage is the tearing away of most or all of the roof. When this happens the walls are no longer adequately supported at the top and are more prone to collapse. Total destruction of a mobile home is more likely if the roof blows off first and then the home overturns. There should be tie-downs over the top to resist overturning and frame ties to prevent sliding off the piers. This applies to single mobile homes up to 14 feet in width. Double-wide mobile homes do not require over-the-top ties, but they do require frame ties. Although newer mobile homes are equipped with built-in straps to aid in tying down, the occupant may wish to add more if the location is particularly vulnerable. Many of the older mobile homes are not equipped with these built-in straps.

Protecting Mobile Homes from High Winds (appendix C) lists specific steps that one should take upon receiving a storm warning and suggests a type of community shelter for a mobile home park.

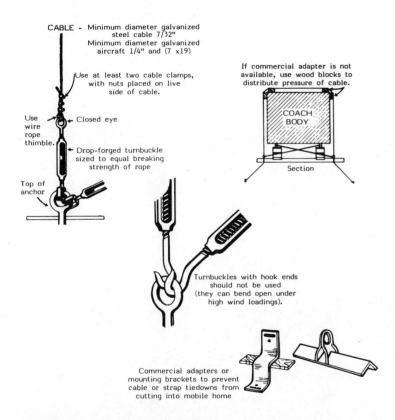

Figure 6.14. Hardware for mobile home tiedowns. (Modified from U.S. Civil Defense Preparedness Agency Publication TR-75.)

Table 6.1   Tiedown anchorage requirements

| | 10- and 12-ft.-wide mobile homes | | | | 12- and 14-ft.-wide mobile homes | |
| | 30 to 50 ft. long | | 50 to 60 ft. long | | 60 to 70 ft. long | |
Wind velocity (mph)	Number of frame ties	Number of over-the-top ties	Number of frame ties	Number of over-the-top ties	Number of frame ties	Number of over-the-top ties
70	3	2	4	2	4	2
80	4	3	5	3	5	3
90	5	4	6	4	7	4
100	6	5	7	5	8	6
110	7	6	9	6	10	7

It also includes a map of the United States with lines that indicate areas subject to the strongest sustained winds. In a great hurricane mobile homes will be destroyed no matter what you do to protect them.

An unending game: only the players change

Hurricane or calm, receding shore or accreting land, storm surge flood or sunny sky, migrating dune or maritime forest, win or lose, the gamble of coastal development will continue. If you choose your site with natural safety in view, follow structural engineering design in construction, and take a generally prudent approach to living at the shore (fig. 6.11), then you become the gambler who knows when to hold them, when to fold them, and when to walk away.

Our goal is to provide guidance to today's and tomorrow's players. This book is not the last or by any means the complete guide to coastal living in Maine, but it should provide a beginning. In the appendixes that follow are additional resources that we hope every reader will pursue.

Appendix A
Storm checklist

Although severe storms along the coast are not an annual occurrence, the wise coastal resident is prepared. Keep this checklist handy for protection of family and property.

When a severe storm threatens

__ Listen for official weather reports.
__ Read your newspaper and listen to radio and television for official announcements.
__ Note the address of the nearest emergency shelter.
__ Know the official evacuation route in advance.
__ Pregnant women, the ill, and the infirm should call a physician for advice.
__ Be prepared to turn off gas, water, and electricity where it enters your home.
__ Fill tubs and containers with water (one quart per person per day).
__ Make sure your car's gas tank is full.
__ Secure your boat. Use long lines to allow for rising water.
__ Secure movable objects on your property:
   __ doors
   __ outdoor furniture
   __ shutters
   __ hoses
   __ gates
   __ garbage cans
   __ bicycles or large sports equipment
   __ barbecues or grills
   __ other

If high winds are forecast

__ Board up or tape windows and glassed areas. Draw drapes and window blinds across windows and glass doors. Remove furniture in their vicinity.
__ Stock adequate supplies:
   __ transistor radio
   __ fresh batteries
   __ canned heat
   __ hammer
   __ boards
   __ pliers
   __ hunting knife
   __ tape
   __ first aid kit
   __ prescribed medicines
   __ water purification tablets

— insect repellent
— gum, candy
— life jackets
— charcoal bucket and
   charcoal
— buckets of sand
— flashlights
— candles
— matches
— nails
— screwdriver
— plastic drop cloths,
   waterproof bags, ties
— containers of water
— disinfectant
— canned food, juices, soft
   drinks (see below)
— hard-top head gear
— fire extinguisher
— can opener and utensils
— Check mobile home tiedowns

Suggested storm food stock for family of four

— two 13-oz. cans evaporated milk
— four 7-oz. cans fruit juice
— two cans tuna, sardines, Spam, chicken

— three 10-oz. cans vegetable soup
— one small can of cocoa or Ovaltine
— one 15-oz. box raisins or prunes
— salt
— pet food?
— one 14-oz. can cream of wheat or oatmeal
— one 8-oz. jar peanut butter or cheese spread
— two 16-oz. cans pork and beans
— one 2-oz. jar instant coffee or tea bags
— two packages of crackers
— two pounds of sugar
— two quarts of water per person

Special precautions for apartments/condominiums

— Make one person the building captain to supervise storm preparation.
— Know your exits.
— Count stairs on exits; you might be evacuating in darkness.
— Locate safest areas for occupants to congregate.
— Close, lock and tape windows.
— Remove loose items from terraces (and from your absent neighbors' terraces).
— Remove or tie down loose objects from balconies or porches.
— Assume other trapped people may wish to use the building for shelter.

Special precautions for mobile homes

__ Pack breakables in padded cartons and place on floor.
__ Remove bulbs, lamps, mirrors. Put them in the bathtub.
__ Tape windows.
__ Turn off water, propane gas, electricity.
__ Disconnect sewer and water lines.
__ Remove awnings.
__ **Leave.**

Special precautions for businesses

__ Take photos of building and merchandise.
__ Assemble insurance policies.
__ Move merchandise away from plate glass.
__ Move merchandise to as high a location as possible.
__ Cover merchandise with tarps or plastic.
__ Remove outside display racks and loose signs.
__ Take out lower file drawers, wrap in trash bags, and store high.
__ Sandbag spaces that may leak.
__ Take special precautions with reactive or toxic chemicals.

If you remain at home

__ Never remain in a mobile home; seek official shelter.
__ Stay indoors. Remain indoors until an official all-clear is given.
__ Keep continuous communications watch for official information on radio and television.

__ Keep calm. Your ability to meet emergencies will help others.
__ Be aware of water levels in your area.

If evacuation is advised

__ Leave as soon as you can. Follow official instructions only.
__ Follow official evacuation routes unless those in authority direct you to do otherwise.
__ Take these supplies:
   __ change of warm, protective clothes
   __ first aid kit
   __ baby formula
   __ identification tags: include name, address, and next of kin (wear them)
   __ flashlight
   __ food, water, gum, candy
   __ rope, hunting knife
   __ waterproof bags and ties
   __ can opener and utensils
   __ disposable diapers
   __ special medicine
   __ blankets and pillows in waterproof casings
   __ radio

— fresh batteries
— bottled water
— purse, wallet, valuables
— life jackets
— games and amusements
  for children
— Disconnect all electric appliances except refrigerator and freezer. Their controls should be turned to the coldest setting and the doors kept closed.
— Leave food and water for pets. Seeing Eye dogs are the only animals allowed in the shelters.
— Shut off water at the main valve (where it enters your home).
— Lock windows and doors.
— Keep important papers with you:
  — driver's license and other
    identification
  — insurance policies
  — property inventory
  — Medic Alert or other
    device to convey special
    medical information.

During the storm

— Stay indoors and away from windows and glassed areas.
— If you are advised to evacuate, **do so at once**.
— Listen for continuing weather bulletins and official reports.

— Use your telephone only in an emergency.
— Follow official instructions only. Ignore rumors.
— Be alert for rising water.
— If electric service is interrupted, note the time.
  — Turn off major
    appliances, especially air
    conditioners.
  — Do not disconnect
    refrigerators or freezers.
    Their controls should be
    turned to the coldest
    setting and doors closed
    to preserve food as long
    as possible.
  — Keep away from fallen
    wires. Report location of
    such wires to the utility
    company.
— If you detect **gas:**
  — Do not light matches or
    turn on electrical
    equipment.
  — Extinguish all flames.
  — Shut off gas supply at the
    meter.*

*Gas should be turned back on only by a gas serviceman or licensed plumber.

___ Report gas service
interruptions to the gas
company.

___ **Water:**

   ___ The only **safe** water is
the water you stored
before it had a chance to
come in contact with
flood waters.

   ___ Should you require an
additional supply, be sure
to boil water for 30
minutes before use.

   ___ If you are unable to boil
water, treat water you
will need with water
purification tablets.

Note: An official announcement will proclaim tap water "safe."
Treat all water except stored water until you hear the announcement.

After the storm has passed

___ Listen for official word of danger having passed.

___ Watch out for loose or hanging power lines as well as gas
leaks. People have survived storms only to be electrocuted or
burned. Fire protection may be nil because of broken power
lines.

___ Walk or drive carefully through the storm-damaged area.
Streets will be dangerous because of debris, undermining by
washout, and weakened bridges.

___ Eat nothing and drink nothing that has been touched by
floodwaters.

___ Place spoiled food in plastic bags and tie securely.

___ Dispose of all mattresses, pillows, and cushions that have been
in floodwaters.

___ Contact relatives as soon as possible.

Note: If you are stranded, signal for help by waving a flashlight at
night or white cloth during the day.

Appendix B

A guide to federal, state, and local agencies involved in coastal development

Numerous agencies at all levels of government are engaged in planning, regulating, or studying coastal development in Maine. These agencies issue permits for various phases of construction and provide information on development to the homeowner, developer, or planner. The following is an alphabetical list of topics related to coastal development; under each topic are the names of agencies to consult for information on that topic.

Aerial photography

Aerial photographs should be available from:

Maine Geological Survey
State House Station 22
Augusta, ME 04333
Phone: (207) 289-2801

J. W. Sewall Company
147 Center Street
Old Town, ME 04468
Phone: (207) 827-4456

U.S. Geological Survey
National Cartographic Information Center
507 National Center
Reston, VA 22092
Phone: (703) 860-6045

Bridges and causeways

The U.S. Coast Guard has jurisdiction over the issuing of permits to build bridges or causeways that will affect navigable waters. Information is available from:

Commander, Bridge Branch [OBR]
1st Coast Guard District
408 Atlantic Avenue
Boston, MA 02212-2209
Phone: (617) 223-8337

Building codes and zoning

Building codes and zoning are controlled locally in Maine. For specific information on this topic contact the local government in the area of interest.

Civil preparedness.

See *Disaster assistance*.

Coastal erosion

Maine Geological Survey
State House Station 22
Augusta, ME 04333
Phone: (207) 289-2801

District Engineer
U.S. Army Corps of Engineers
424 Trapelo Road
Waltham, MA 02254
Phone: (617) 647-8528

Coastal Zone Management Act, Maine

The Maine Coastal Zone Management Program is administered
as a section of the state Department of Environmental Protection.
Some towns have chosen to participate and are involved in issues
of local concern (such as development). For information contact
the office below and the local government.

Shoreland Zoning Coordinator
Department of Environmental Protection
State House Station 17
Augusta, ME 04333
Phone: (207) 289-2111

Disaster assistance

For information, call or write:

Coordinator
Federal Emergency Management Agency
State Planning Office
State House Station 38
Augusta, ME 04333
Phone: (207) 289-3261

American National Red Cross
Disaster Services
Washington, DC 20006
Phone: (207) 857-3722

Dredging, filling, and construction in coastal waterways

Federal law requires that any person who wishes to dredge, fill,
or place any structure in navigable water (almost any body of
water) apply for a permit from the U.S. Army Corps of Engineers.
Information is available from:

District Engineer
U.S. Army Corps of Engineers
424 Trapelo Road
Waltham, MA 02254

Land Bureau
Department of Environmental Protection
State House Station 17
Augusta, ME 04333
(207) 289-2111

Geologic information

You may request geologic and water supply reports and maps, and a free index map from:

Distribution Section
U.S. Geological Survey
Federal Center
Denver, CO 80225

Similar information is also available from:

Maine Geological Survey
State House Station 22
Augusta, ME 04333
Phone: (207) 289-2801

Literature describing natural barrier islands is available from:

Office of Ocean and Coastal Resource Management
National Oceanic and Atmospheric Administration
3300 Whitehaven Street, N.W.
Washington, DC 20235

Hazards. *See also* Coastal erosion and insurance.

Coordinator
Federal Emergency Management Agency
State Planning Office
State House Station 38
Augusta, ME 04333
Phone: (207) 289-3261

History

Maine Historic Preservation Commission
State House Station 65
Augusta, ME 04333
Phone: (207) 289-2132

Local libraries also may be helpful, especially for copies of micro-films of newspapers. Additional information of interest may be found in the Maine collection of the libraries of the University of Maine and the University of Southern Maine.

Hurricane information

The National Oceanic and Atmospheric Administration is the best agency from which to request information on hurricanes. NOAA storm evacuation maps are prepared for vulnerable areas. To find out whether a map for your area is available, call or write:

Distribution Division (C-44)
National Ocean Survey
National Oceanic and Atmospheric Administration
Riverdale, MD 20840
Phone: (301) 436-6990

Insurance

In coastal areas special building requirements must often be met in order to obtain flood or windstorm insurance. To find out the requirements for a specific area, contact a local insurance agent.

Further information is available from:

State Coordinating Agency for Flood Insurance
State Planning Office
State House Station 38
Augusta, ME 04333
Phone: (207) 289-3261

National Flood Insurance Program
Federal Insurance Administration
Federal Emergency Management Agency
Washington, DC 20472

Information on V zone coverage and individual structure rating is available from:

National Flood Insurance Program
Attn: V zone Underwriting Specialist
P.O. Box 34653
Bethesda, MD 20817
Phone: (800) 638-6620 (toll-free)

Maps

A wide variety of maps is useful to planners and managers and may be of interest to individual property owners. Topographic, geologic, and land use maps, as well as orthophoto quadrangles, are available from:

Distribution Section
U.S. Geological Survey
Federal Center, Box 25286
Denver, CO 80225

Maine Geological Survey
State House Station 22
Augusta, ME 04333
Phone: (207) 289-2801

County highway maps are available from:

State Department of Transportation
State House Station 16
Augusta, ME 04333
Phone: (207) 289-2551

Information on how to obtain flood maps of a community is available from:

Coordinator
FEMA
State Planning Office
State House Station 38
Augusta, ME 04333
Phone: (207) 289-3261

National Flood Insurance Program
P.O. Box 34294
Bethesda, MD 20034

Nautical charts: a nautical chart index map is available from:

National Ocean Survey
Distribution Division (C-44)
National Oceanic and Atmospheric Administration
Riverdale, MD 20840
Phone: (301) 436-6990

Planning maps: call or write the local county or town government.
Soil maps: see *Soils*.

Marine and coastal zone educational information

Maine has done little, compared to other states, to educate the public on the coastline. The following organizations are the best sources of such information:

Maine Audubon Society
118 Route 1
Falmouth, ME 04105
Phone: (207) 781-2330

I. C. Darling Center
Walpole, ME 04573
Phone: (207) 563-3146

Center for Marine Studies
Sea Grant Office
University of Maine
Orono, ME 04469
Phone: (207) 581-1436

Parks and recreation

Bureau of Parks and Recreation
State House Station 19
Augusta, ME 04333
Phone: (207) 289-3821

Planning and land use

Director
Land Bureau
Department of Environmental Protection
State House Station 17
Augusta, ME 04333
Phone: (207) 289-2111

State Planning Office
State House Station 38
Augusta, ME 04333
Phone: (207) 289-3261

For specific information check with the local town or county government. Many local governments have planning boards and have available copies of existing or proposed land use plans.

Remote sensing imagery

Information on remote sensing imagery is available from:

U.S. Geological Survey
National Cartographic Information Center (NSTL)
Building 1100, Room 218
NSTL Station
Bay St. Louis, MS 39529
Phone: (601) 688-3544

Roads and property access

Be sure that access rights and roads will be provided before buying property. Permits may be needed to connect driveways to state-maintained roads. For further information contact:

Department of Transportation
State House Station 16
Augusta, ME 04333
Phone: (207) 289-2551

Sanitation

Before construction can begin permits must be obtained for waste treatment and discharge. For information contact the following agency:

Director
Land Bureau
Department of Environmental Protection
State House Station 17
Augusta, ME 04333
Phone: (207) 289-2111

A permit for the construction of a sewage disposal or any other structure in navigable waters must be obtained from the U.S. Army Corps of Engineers. More information is available from:

Permits and Statistics Branch
U.S. Army Corps of Engineers
New England Division
424 Trapelo Road
Waltham, MA 02254
Phone: (207) 647-8528

A permit for any discharge into navigable waters must be obtained from the U.S. Environmental Protection Agency. Recent judicial interpretation of the federal Water Pollution Control Amendments of 1972 extends federal jurisdiction for protection of wetlands above the mean high water mark. Federal permits may

now be required for the development of land that occasionally is flooded by water draining indirectly into a navigable waterway.
Information may be obtained from:

Environmental Protection Agency
JFK Federal Building
Boston, MA 02117
Phone: (617) 565-3715

Septic system information and permits.
See Sanitation.

Soils

Soil type is important for the type of vegetation it can support, the type of construction technique it can withstand, its drainage characteristics, and its ability to accommodate septic systems. For information contact:

U.S. Department of Agriculture
Soil Conservation Service
USDA Building
University of Maine
Orono, ME 04469
Phone: (207) 866-2132

Also check with the local Soil and Water Conservation District office.

Subdivisions

Subdivisions containing more than 100 lots and offered in interstate commerce must be registered with the Office of Interstate Land Sales Registration (as specified by the Interstate Land Sales Full Disclosure Act). Prospective buyers must be provided with a property report. This office also produces a booklet entitled "Get The Facts . . . Before Buying Land" for people who wish to invest in land. Information on subdivision property and land investment is available from:

Office of Interstate Land Sales Registration
Atlanta Regional Office
U.S. Department of Housing and Urban Development
230 Peachtree Street, N.W.
Atlanta, GA 30303
Phone: (404) 526-4364

Vegetation

Information on vegetation may be obtained from the local Soil and Water Conservation District office.

Water resources. *See also* Dredging and Sanitation.

A variety of agencies are concerned with water quality and availability. Information can be obtained from the following:

Department of Inland Fisheries and Wildlife
State House Station 41
Augusta, ME 04333
Phone: (207) 289-3371

Department of Marine Resources
State House Station 21
Augusta, ME 04333
Phone: (207) 289-2291

Appendix C.
Useful references

The following publications are listed by subject; subjects are arranged in the approximate order that they appear in the preceding chapters. A brief description of each reference is provided, and sources are included for those readers who would like to obtain more information on a particular subject. Some publications are listed as available only in university libraries. Readers without direct access to a university library should ask their local public library about the possibility of obtaining these materials through interlibrary loan. Most of the documents listed are either low in cost or free; we encourage the reader to take advantage of these informative publications.

Coastal Environment and Hazard Maps, by Stephen M. Dickson, 1988. A set of 38 large-scale maps of Maine's major sand beaches. These depict the geological environments, hazards, and suitability for development of the beaches on a lot-by-lot basis. Deemed the "best available data" by the State Board of Environmental Protection, these are essential reading for the prospective buyer. Available from the Maine Geological Survey, State House Station 22, Augusta, ME 04333.

History and geography

1. *Islands of Maine*, by Bill Caldwell, 1981. Readable description of the history of Maine's islands. Published by Guy Gannet Publishing Co., Portland, ME. Commonly available in libraries.

2. *The Coast of Maine—An Informal History*, by L. D. Rich, 1970. An older account of the history and geography of coastal Maine. Published by T. Y. Crowell Co., New York, NY. Commonly available in libraries.

3. *The Maine Atlas and Gazetteer*, 1983. A compilation of maps covering the entire state of Maine. Bound in easy-to-use book form. Brief descriptions of sites of historic and scenic interest are included. Published by DeLorme Publishing Co., Freeport, ME. Available in bookstores throughout Maine.

4. *Coastal Marine Geologic Maps*, by Barry Timson, 1977. Highly detailed, 1:24,000 maps of coastal environments along the entire tidally influenced shoreline of Maine. Available from the Maine Geological Survey, State House Station 22, Augusta, ME 04333.

5. *The Coastal Almanac*, by P. L. Ringold and J. Clark, 1980. Contains more than 150 pages of statistics on the use of the American coast. Published by W. H. Freeman and Co., 660 Market Street, San Francisco, CA 94104.

Storms

6. *Early American Hurricanes, 1492–1870*, by D. M. Ludlum, 1963. Informative and entertaining descriptions of storms affecting

the Atlantic and Gulf coasts. Storm accounts in chronological order provide insight into the frequency, intensity, and destructive potential of hurricanes. Published by the American Meteorological Society, Boston. Available in public and university libraries.

7. *Atlantic Hurricanes*, by G. E. Dunn and B. I. Miller, 1960. Discusses at length hurricanes and associated phenomena such as storm surge, wind, and sea action. Includes a detailed account of Hurricane Hazel, 1954, and suggestions for pre- and post-hurricane procedures. An appendix includes a list of hurricanes for the Carolinas. Published by Louisiana State University Press, Baton Rouge, LA. Available in public and college libraries.

8. *Hurricane Information and Atlantic Tracking Chart*, by the National Oceanic and Atmospheric Administration, 1974. A brochure that describes hurricanes, defines terms, and lists hurricane safety rules. Outlines the method of tracing hurricanes and provides a tracking map. Available from the Superintendent of Documents, U.S. Government Printing Office, Washington, DC 20402.

9. *Hurricanes*, by I. R. Tannehill, 1950. A discussion of the causes of tropical storms followed by fascinating anecdotal accounts of major hurricanes. Published by Princeton University Press, Princeton, NJ.

10. *Great Storms and Famous Shipwrecks of the New England Coast*, by Edward R. Snow, 1944. Anecdotal coverage of major storms and the damage they caused along the New England coast.

Geology and oceanography

11. *An Ecological Characterization of Coastal Maine*, by S. I. Fefer and P. Shettig, 1980. An extraordinary compilation of maps and tables with complementary text on the coast of Maine north of Portland. There are many volumes in this almanac, and it is available only in large libraries. Published by the U.S. Fish and Wildlife Service, Newton Corner, MA.

12. *Bedrock Geologic Map of Maine*, by P. H. Osberg, A. M. Hussey II, and G. M. Boone, 1985. A 1:500,000 map of the entire state with numerous smaller maps and an extensive bibliography. Published by Maine Geological Survey, Augusta, ME 04333.

13. *Surficial Geologic Map of Maine*, by W. B. Thompson and H. W. Borns, Jr., 1985. A 1:500,000 map of the glacial and modern deposits of the state with depictions of the glacial history, a listing of interesting sites, and a thorough bibliography. Published by the Maine Geological Survey, Augusta, ME 04333.

14. *The Gulf of Maine*, by Spencer Apollonio, 1979. A thoroughly interesting and highly readable description of the origin, evolution, and processes acting in this rich fishery bounding the Maine coast. Available at many bookstores. Published by Courier Gazette, Inc., Rockland, ME.

15. *The Geology of Maine's Coastline*, by the Maine State Planning Office, 1983. A booklet intended to accompany the Coastal Marine Geologic Maps by Timson (entry 4). Available from the State Planning Office, Augusta, ME 04333.

16. "Sedimentary Environments Along Maine's Estuarine Coastline", by Joseph T. Kelley, 1987, in *A Treatise on Glaciated Coasts*, D. FitzGerald and P. Rosen (eds.), Academic Press, Orlando, FL. A highly technical summary of the abundance of various environments along the Maine coast. Available only in large libraries.

17. *Surficial Geology Handbook for Coastal Maine*, by Woodrow B. Thompson, 1979. A nongeologist's guide to Ice Age features along the Maine coastal region. Available from the State Planning Office, Augusta, ME, and larger libraries.

18. "Variability in the Evolution of Two Adjacent Bedrock-Framed Estuaries in Maine," by J. T. Kelley, A. R. Kelley, D. F. Belknap, and R. C. Shipp, 1986, in *Estuarine Variability*, D. Wolfe (ed.), Academic Press, Orlando, FL, pp. 21–42. A technical account of why Saco Bay (Old Orchard) is geologically different from Casco Bay (Portland). Available only in large libraries.

19. *Coastal Processes and Quaternary Stratigraphy: Northern and Central Coastal Maine*, by Joseph T. Kelley and Alice Kelley (eds.), 1986. A field guide, with numerous maps and photographs, to the geology of the least well-known portion of the Maine coast. Available from SEPM, Eastern Section, William Sevon, Pennsylvania Geological Survey, Harrisburg, PA.

20. *Glaciers and Granite*, by David L. Kendall, 1987. A general discussion of the geology of the state of Maine. Available from Down East Books, Camden, ME, or libraries.

21. "Present Coastal Processes, Recorded Changes, and the Post-Pleistocene Geologic Record of Saco Bay, Maine," by Stewart C. Farrell, 1972. A compilation of vintage maps from the Saco Bay area and an extended technical discussion of the geological processes at work there. Unpublished Ph.D. dissertation, University of Massachusetts, Amherst, MA. Available from University Microfilms International, 300 North Zeeb Road, Ann Arbor, MI 48106.

Barrier beaches

22. *Barrier Island Atlas of the Atlantic and Gulf Coasts*, 1980. A summary of land use statistics on America's barrier islands. Available as Professional Paper 1156 from the U.S. Geological Survey, 604 South Pickett Street, Alexandria, VA 22304.

23. *Waves and Beaches*, by Willard Bascom, 1964. A discussion of beaches and coastal processes. Published by Anchor Books, Doubleday and Co., Garden City, NY 11530. Available in paperback from local bookstores.

24. *Beaches and Coasts*, 2d ed., by C. A. M. King, 1972. Classic treatment of beach and coastal processes. Published by St. Martin's Press, 175 Fifth Avenue, New York, NY 10010.

25. *Beach Processes and Sedimentation*, by Paul Komar, 1976. The most up-to-date technical explanations of beaches and beach processes. Recommended only to serious students of the beach. Published by Prentice-Hall, Englewood Cliffs, NJ 07632.

26. *Geological and Botanical Features of Sand Beach Systems in Maine*, by B. W. Nelson and L. K. Fink, 1980. A moderately

technical description of the interesting geology and botany to be found on sandy beaches. The book also introduces the reader to the geological processes that maintain Maine's beaches. Published by the Maine Sea Grant Program, Center for Marine Studies, University of Maine, Orono, ME 04469.

27. "Shoreline Changes and Physiography of Maine's Sandy Coastal Beaches," by Bruce W. Nelson, 1979. A useful documentation of the amount of change Maine's sandy beaches have undergone. Available only at the University of Maine Library as an unpublished master's thesis.

Marshes and estuaries

28. *Life and Death of the Salt Marsh*, by John and Mildred Teal, 1969. Written about a New England marsh, this is a very readable account of life within a marsh and man's influence on wetlands. Published by Audubon/Ballantine Books, New York.

29. "Coastal Salt Marshes," by R. W. Frey and P. B. Basan, 1985, in *Coastal Sedimentary Environments*, R. A. Davis (ed.), Springer Verlag, New York, pp. 225–301. A thorough technical review on current research in marshes with many useful references. Available in university libraries.

30. *The Ecology of New England High Salt Marshes*, by Scott Nixon, 1982. A detailed compendium on what is known of (mostly southern) New England's salt marshes. Available in large libraries and produced by the U.S. Fish and Wildlife Service as publication US FLUS/BS-81-55.

31. *Intertidal Bedrock Areas of High Species Diversity in Maine*, by Lee Doggett, Peter Larson, and Susan Sykes. A description of the numerous organisms inhabiting rocky coastlines. Available from the State Planning Office, Augusta, ME 04333.

32. *The Ecology of Maine's Intertidal Habitats*, by Peter Larson and Lee Doggett, 1981. A complete description of the diverse habitats of Maine's intertidal regions and the organisms living there. Available from the State Planning Office, Augusta, ME 04333.

33. "Distribution and Abundance of Tidal Marshes Along the Coast of Maine," by G. L. Jacobson, H. A. Jacobson, and J. T. Kelley, 1987, in *Estuaries*, vol. 10, pp. 126–31. Contains maps and graphs showing the extent of Maine's salt marshes. Available in larger libraries.

Coastal engineering

34. *Shore Protection Guidelines*, by the U.S. Army Corps of Engineers, 1971. Summary of the effects of waves, tides, and winds on beaches and engineering structures used for beach stabilization. Available free from the Corps of Engineers, Department of the Army, Washington, DC 20318.

35. *Shore Protection Manual*, by the U.S. Army Corps of Engineers, 1984. The "bible" of shoreline engineering. Published in two volumes. Request publication 008-022-00218-9 from the Superintendent of Documents, U.S. Government Printing Office, Washington, DC 20402.

36. *Help Yourself*, by the U.S. Army Corps of Engineers. Brochure addressing the erosion problems in the Great Lakes region. May be of interest to barrier island residents as it outlines shoreline processes and illustrates a variety of shoreline engineering devices used to combat erosion. Free from the U.S. Army Corps of Engineers, North Central Division, 219 South Dearborn Street, Chicago, IL 60604.

37. *Coastal Hydraulics*, by A. M. Muir Wood, 1969. A shoreline engineering textbook suitable for engineering students. Published by Gordon and Breach Science Publishers, 150 Fifth Avenue, New York, NY 10011.

38. *Bibliography of Publications Prior to July 1983 of the Coastal Engineering Research Center and the Beach Erosion Board*, by A. Szuwalski and S. Wagner, 1984. A list of published coastal research by the U.S. Army Corps of Engineers. Available free from the Coastal Engineering Research Center, U.S. Army Engineer Waterways Experiment Station, P.O. Box 631, Vicksburg, MS 39180.

39. *List of Publications of the U.S. Army Engineer Waterways Experiment Station, Volumes I and II*, by R. M. Peck, 1984 and 1985. Updates entry 38; also lists publications by other research branches of the Waterways Experiment Station. Available free from the Special Projects Branch, Technical Information Center, U.S. Army Engineers Waterways Experiment Station, P.O. Box 631, Vicksburg, MS 39180.

40. *Beach Nourishment Along the Southeast Atlantic and Gulf Coasts*, by Todd Walton and James Purpura, 1977, in *Shore and Beach* magazine (July), pp. 10–18. Examines successes and failures of several beach nourishment projects, including the rapid postnourishment losses of beach fill at Hunting Island, South Carolina.

41. *Beach Behavior in the Vicinity of Groins*, by C. H. Everts, 1979. A description of the effects of two groin fields in New Jersey, which concludes that groins cause erosion in the downdrift shadow area. Published in the Proceedings of the Specialty Conference on Coastal Structures 79 (pp. 853–67) and available as reprint 79-3 from the U.S. Army Coastal Engineering Research Center, Vicksburg, MS.

42. *Low-Cost Shore Protection*, by the U.S. Army Corps of Engineers, 1982. A set of four reports written for the layperson under this title includes an introductory report, a property owner's guide, a guide for local government officials, and a guide for engineers and contractors. The reports are a summary of the Shoreline Erosion Control Demonstration Program and suggest a wide range of engineering devices and techniques to stabilize shorelines, including beach nourishment and vegetation. In adopting these approaches, you should keep in mind that they are short-term measures and may have unwanted side effects. The reports are available from Section 54 Program, U.S. Army Corps of Engineers, USACE (DAEN-CWP-F), Washington, DC 20314.

43. *Responding to Changes in Sea Level, Engineering Implications*, by the Committee on Engineering Implications of Changes in Relative Mean Sea Level of the Marine Board Commission on Engineering and Technical Systems, National Research Council,

1987. This technical reference is of interest to community planners, officials, and legislators because of the implications of the sea level rise for all coastal development. Although no specific solutions are provided, the text does conclude with some relevant general recommendations. For sale by the National Academy Press, 2101 Constitution Avenue, N.W., Washington, DC 20418.

Recreation

44. *Fifty Hikes in Maine*, by John Gibson, 1986. This book includes a section on day hikes in the Camden area, Mount Desert Island, and Isle Au Haut. Published by Backcountry Publications, Inc., Woodstock, Vermont. Widely available in bookstores and in some libraries.

45. *Maine Forever: A Guide to Nature Conservancy Preserves in Maine*, by Mary Minor C. S. Lannon, 1984. Descriptions of Nature Conservancy holdings in Maine, many of which are along the coast or on islands. The text includes descriptions of hiking trails and maps. Available from the Maine chapter, the Nature Conservancy, 20 Federal Street, Brunswick, ME 04011. Also available in some bookstores.

Hazards

46. *Guidelines for Identifying Coastal High Hazard Zones*, by the U.S. Army Corps of Engineers, 1975. Report outlining such zones with emphasis on "coastal special flood-hazard areas" (coastal floodplains subject to inundation by storm surge with a 1 percent chance of occurring in any given year). Provides technical guidelines for conducting uniform flood insurance studies and outlines methods of obtaining 100-year storm surge elevations. Recommended to beach planners. Available from the Galveston District, U.S. Army Corps of Engineers, Galveston, TX 77553.

47. *Shoreline Waves, Another Energy Crisis*, by Victor Goldsmith, 1975. Shows how the depth of water along and out from the beach affects wave height. Suggests that wave energy distribution may be controlled. Free from Sea Grant College Program, Virginia Institute of Marine Science, Gloucester Point, VA 23062. Request VIMS contribution no. 734.

48. *Natural Hazard Management in Coastal Areas*, by G. F. White and others, 1976. The most recent summary of coastal hazards along the entire U.S. coast. Discusses adjustments to such hazards and hazard-related federal policy and programs. Summarizes hazard management and coastal land planning programs in each state. Appendixes include a directory of agencies, an annotated bibliography, and information on hurricanes. An invaluable reference, recommended to developers, planners, and managers. Available from the Office of Ocean and Coastal Resource Management, National Oceanic and Atmospheric Administration, 3300 Whitehaven Street, N.W., Washington, DC 20235.

Natural history

49. *Beach Vegetation and Oceanic Processes: A Study of Popham Beach State Park, Reid Beach State Park, and Small Point Beach*, by P. Trudeau, 1977. A botanical study of dune communities at three accessible and relatively undisturbed locations. Available from Maine Department of Conservation, Augusta, ME.

50. *Vegetation Patterns and Processes in New England Salt Marshes*, by W. Niering and R. Warren, 1980, in *Bioscience* 30:301–7. Discusses the way coastal processes operate to influence plant communities in marshes. Available only in large libraries.

51. *Beachcomber's Botany*, by Loren C. Petry, 1968. Although this book was intended as a guide to the plants of the Cape Cod area, it is quite applicable to Maine. Beautifully illustrated with pencil sketches. Available in libraries and from the Chatham Conservation Foundation, Inc., Box 317, Chatham, MA 02633.

52. *Atlantic and Gulf Coasts*, by William H. Amos and Stephen H. Amos, 1985. This is one in the series of Audubon Society nature guides. Although many detailed guides to the flora and fauna of the coast exist, this book covers each of the major categories: geology, shells, seashore animals, mammals, fishes, reptiles and amphibians, plants, insects and spiders, and birds. Published by Alfred A. Knopf, New York. Available in libraries and bookstores.

53. *The Maine Coast: A Nature Lover's Guide*, by Dorcas Miller, 1979. Discusses the flora and fauna of the Maine coast in easy-to-read terms. Also includes a description of coastal sites of interest to the naturalist. Available from East Woods Books, 429 East Kingston Avenue, Charlotte, NC 28203, and libraries.

Archaeology

54. *Discovering Maine's Archeological Heritage*, by David Sanger, 1979. A series of papers that serve as an introduction to the archaeology of Maine, both prehistoric and historic. Coastal sites are discussed. Published by the Maine Historic Preservation Commission in Augusta. This book is currently out of print but is available through libraries.

55. *The Archaeology of New England*, by Dean R. Snow, 1980. The scope of this book is all of New England, but it does contain discussions of the prehistory of Maine. Published by Academic Press, New York. Available through libraries.

Site analysis

56. *Handbook: Building in the Coastal Environment*, by R. T. Segrest and Associates, 1975. A well-illustrated, clearly and simply written book on Georgia coastal zone planning, construction, and selling problems. Topics include vegetation, soil, drainage, setback requirements, access, climate, and building orientation. Includes a list of addresses for agencies and other sources of information. Much of the information applies to Maine. Available from the Graphics Department, Coastal Area Planning and Development Commission, P.O. Box 1316, Brunswick, GA 31520.

Water problems

57. *Your Home Septic System, Success or Failure?* Brochure providing answers to commonly asked questions on home septic systems. Lists agencies that supply information on septic tank installation and operation. Available from UNC Sea Grant, 1235 Burlington Laboratories, North Carolina State University, Raleigh, NC 27607.

58. *Report of Investigation of the Environmental Effects of Private Waterfront Lands*, by W. Barada and W. M. Partington, 1972. An enlightening reference that treats the effects of finger canals on water quality. Available from the Environmental Information Center, the Florida Conservation Foundation, Inc., 935 Orange Avenue, Winter Park, FL 32789.

59. *The Groundwater Handbook for the State of Maine*, by W. B. Caswell, 1979. The primary reference for finding out about groundwater in coastal Maine. Available from the Maine Geological Survey, State House Station 22, Augusta, ME 04333.

60. *Maine Coastal Area Water Supply and Demand*, by W. B. Caswell, 1979. A report with accompanying atlas on coastal needs and resources. Available from the Maine Geological Survey, Augusta, ME 04333.

61. *Answers to Questions About the Safe Drinking Water Act*. Provides answers to questions about your tap water. Obtain a copy from the regional office of the U.S. Environmental Protection Agency. There are also several pamphlets available from the National Water Institute. These include *How About the Water*, *Background on Water Pollution*, and *Water Is a Manufactured Product*. To obtain these pamphlets contact the National Water Institute, Room 3405, 744 Broad Street, Newark, NJ 07102.

Specific coastal areas

62. *History of Sedimentation in Montsweag Bay*, by Detmar Schnitker, 1972. The only detailed geological study to date of a large portion of an estuary. Available from the Maine Geological Survey, State House Station 22, Augusta, ME 04333.

63. *Geomorphologic Trends in a Glaciated Coastal Bay: A Model for the Maine Coast*, by R. Craig Shipp, Stephanie A. Staples, and Walter H. Adey, 1985. A thorough description of the evolution and geological environments of Gouldsboro Bay. Available from Smithsonian Institution Press, Washington, DC, as Marine Contribution 25.

64. *Geology of Mt. Desert Island*, by Richard A. Gilman, Carleton A. Chapman, Thomas V. Lowell, and Harold W. Borns, Jr., 1987. A modern and comprehensive guide to the bedrock and glacial geology of this famous island. Available from the Maine Geological Survey, State House Station 22, Augusta, ME, as bulletin no. 38.

65. *Geomorphology and Sedimentary Framework of the Inner Continental Shelf of Southwestern Maine*, by J. Kelley, R. Shipp, D. Belknap, 1986, and *Geomorphology and Sedimentary Framework of the Inner Continental Shelf of South Central Maine*,

by J. Kelley, R. Shipp, D. Belknap, 1986. Each of these volumes deals exhaustively with evolution of the seafloor in estuaries and along the inner shelf. Available from the Maine Geological Survey, Augusta, ME, as Open File Reports 87-5 and 87-19, respectively.

66. "Depositional Setting and Quaternary Stratigraphy of the Sheepscot Estuary, Maine: A Preliminary Report," by Daniel Belknap, R. Shipp, and J. Kelley, 1986. A technical report available at university libraries in *Geographie Physique et Quaternaire*, vol. 40, pp. 55–69.

Conservation and planning

67. *Coastal Management: Planning on the Edge*, edited by D. R. Godschalk and Kathryn Cousins, 1985. This special issue of the *Journal of the American Planning Association* (vol. 51, no. 3) focuses on coastal management issues and is of interest to community planners, officials, and legislators. Available through larger college and university libraries.

68. *The Water's Edge: Critical Problems of the Coastal Zone*, edited by B. H. Ketchum, 1972. The best available scientific summary of coastal zone problems. Published by the MIT Press, Cambridge, MA 02139.

69. *Design with Nature*, by Ian McHarg, 1969. A classic text on the environment. Stresses that when man interacts with nature, he must recognize its processes and governing laws and realize that it both presents opportunities for and requires limitations on human use. Published by Doubleday and Co., Garden City, NY 11530.

70. *Coastal Ecosystems: Ecological Considerations for Management of the Coastal Zone*, by John Clark, 1974. A clearly written, well-illustrated book applying the principles of ecology to the major coastal zone environments. Available from the publications department of the Conservation Foundation, 1717 Massachusetts Avenue, N.W., Washington, DC 20036.

71. *A Long-Term Dune Management Plan: Old Orchard Beach*, by Barry Timson and Mary Denison, 1986. A thoughtful analysis of the problems involved in managing sand dunes in the state's largest resort town. Available in the town of Old Orchard.

72. *Permits for Activities in Navigable Waters and Ocean Waters*, by the U.S. Army Corps of Engineers, 1975. Description of rules and regulations for processing permits for activities in navigable waters and ocean waters. Published in the *Federal Register*, vol. 40, no. 144, pt. 4.

73. *Protecting Your Coastal Wetlands*, by the Maine Department of Environmental Protection, 1987. A description of Maine's coastal wetlands, their importance, and the state laws that apply to development in the coastal zone. Available from the Department of Environmental Protection, State House Station 17, Augusta, ME 04333.

74. *Preparing for Hurricanes and Coastal Flooding: A Handbook for Local Officials*, by Ralph M. Field Associates, 1983. A comprehensive handbook, valuable for all phases of local, county, and state planning for coastal storms. Available from the Federal Emergency Management Agency.

75. *Perspectives on Hurricane Preparedness*, by the Federal

Emergency Management Agency. This booklet, designed for government planners, highlights the successful efforts of various state and local governments to raise the level of citizen preparedness. Available from the Federal Emergency Management Agency.

76. *After the Storm: Perpetuating the Folly of Coastal Development*, by the Natural Resources Defense Council. This pamphlet describes the federal programs that allow a community to rebuild after a storm. The suggestions point to opportunities for public involvement that could lead to wiser coastal disaster policies. Available from the Natural Resources Defense Council, 122 East 42nd Street, New York, NY 10168.

77. *And Two if by Sea: Fighting the Attack on America's Coast*, by Beth Millemann, 1986. Subtitled "A Citizen's Guide to the Coastal Zone Management Act and Other Coastal Laws," this pocket-sized text is a primer on coastal hazards, pollution, resource development, and ocean dumping. Available from the Coast Alliance, 218 D Street, S.E., Washington, DC 20003.

78. *Ocean and Coastal Law*, by Richard Hildreth and Ralph Johnson, 1983. Discusses (1) problems posed by earlier nonmanagement of public resources and the gradual public awakening to the need for a comprehensive legal framework for the coastal zone, (2) ownership and boundary questions, (3) state common law, (4) offshore issues, (5) alteration of waterways and wetlands, and (6) federal and state coastal zone management programs. For anyone with a serious interest in legal issues. Published by Prentice-Hall, Englewood Cliffs, NJ 07632.

79. "Coastal Natural Hazards Management," by Richard Hildreth, 1980. Presents a good overview of legal issues involved in present and proposed regulatory responses to coastal natural hazards. A fine reference for planners and property owners alike. Published in the *Oregon Law Review*, vol. 59, University of Oregon, Eugene, OR 97403.

80. *Coastal Mapping Handbook*, edited by M. Y. Ellis, 1978. A primer on coastal mapping that outlines the various types of maps, charts, and photography available; sources for such products; data and uses; and state coastal mapping programs. Includes appendixes and examples. A valuable starting reference for anyone interested in maps or mapping. For sale by the Superintendent of Documents, U.S. Government Printing Office, Washington, DC 20402 (stock no. 024-001-03046-2).

Legislation

The following are specific references to the federal legislation mentioned in chapter 5. The first reference indicates where these can be found in the *United States Code*. The second refers to their place in *Statutes at Large*.

81. National Flood Insurance Act of 1968 (P.L. 90–448), enacted on August 1, 1968. (1) 42 U.S.C. sect. 4001 et seq. (1976). (2) 82 Stat. 476, Title 13.

82. Coastal Zone Management Act of 1972 (P.L. 92–583), enacted on October 27, 1972. (1) 16 U.S.C. sect. 1451 et seq. (1976). (2) 82 Stat. 1280. This act has been amended on January 2, 1975 (P.L. 93–612; 16 U.S.C. sects. 1454, 1455, and 1464; 88

Stat. 1974) and on July 26, 1976 (Coastal Zone Management Act Amendments of 1976, P.L. 94–370; 5 U.S.C. sect. 5316, 15 U.S.C. sect. 1511a, and 16 U.S.C. sects. 1451 and 1453–1464; 90 Stat. 1013). Federal Water Pollution Control Act Amendments of 1972 (P.L. 92–500), enacted on October 18, 1972. (1) 33 U.S.C. sect. 1251 et seq. (1976). (2) 86 Stat. 816.

83. Marine Protection, Research, and Sanctuaries Act of 1972 (P.L. 92–532), enacted on October 23, 1972. (1) 33 U.S.C. sect. 1401 et seq. (1976). (2) 86 Stat. 1052.

84. Flood Disaster Protection Act of 1973 (P.L. 92–234), enacted on December 31, 1973. (1) U.S.C. sect. 4001 et seq. (1976). (2) 87 Stat. 975.

85. Water Resources Development Act of 1974 (P.L. 92–251), enacted on March 7, 1974. (1) 16 U.S.C. sects. 4601–13, 4601–14, and 460ee (1976); 22 U.S.C. sect. 275a (1976); 33 U.S.C. sects. 59c-2, 59k, 579, 701b–11, 701g, 701n, 701r, 701r-1, 701s, 709a, 1252a, and 1293a (1976); 42 U.S.C. sects. 1962d-5c, 1962d-15, 1962d-16, and 1962d-17 (1976). (2) 88 Stat. 13, Title I.

86. Coastal Barrier Resources Act (P.L. 97–348), enacted on October 18, 1982. (1) 16 U.S.C. sect. 3501 et seq. (2) 96 Stat. 1653.

Home Construction

87. *Coastal Design: A Guide for Builders, Planners, and Home-owners*, by Orrin H. Pilkey, Jr., Orrin H. Pilkey, Sr., Walter D. Pilkey, and W. J. Neal, 1983. A detailed companion volume and construction guide expanding on the information outlined in this text. Chapters include discussions of shoreline types, individual residence construction, making older structures storm-worthy, high-rise buildings, mobile homes, coastal regulations, and the future of the coastal zone. Published by Van Nostrand Reinhold Company, New York.

88. *Coastal Construction Manual*, prepared by Dames and Moore, and Bliss and Nyitray, Inc., for the Federal Emergency Management Agency, 1986. A guide to the coastal environment with recommendations on site and structure design relative to the National Flood Insurance Program. The report includes design considerations, examples, construction costs, and appendixes on design tables, bracing, design worksheets, wood preservatives, and a listing of useful references. The manual is available from the Superintendent of Documents, U.S. Government Printing Office, Washington, DC 20402 (publication number 620-214/40618), or contact a FEMA office and request FEMA publication no. 55.

89. *Design Guidelines for Flood Damage Reduction*, prepared by the American Institute of Architects for the Federal Emergency Management Agency, 1981.

90. *Flood Emergency and Residential Repair Handbook*, prepared by the National Association of Homebuilders Research Advisory Board of the National Academy of Science, 1986, and available from FEMA as publication no. FIA-13. Guide to flood-proofing as well as step-by-step cleanup procedures and repairs, including household goods and appliances. Available from the Superintendent of Documents, U.S. Government Printing Office,

Washington, DC 20402 (order stock no. 023-000-00552-2), or from FEMA, P.O. Box 8181, Washington, DC 20024.

91. *The Uniform Building Code*. Available from the International Conference of Building Officials, 5360 South Workman Mill Road, Whittier, CA 90601.

92. "Hurricane Exposes Structure Flaws," by Herbert S. Saffir. In *Civil Engineering* magazine, February 1971, pp. 54–55. Available from most university libraries.

93. *Potential Wind Damage Reduction Through the Use of Wind-Resistant Building Standards*. Should be of interest to builders of new structures. Available from the Texas Coastal and Marine Council, P.O. Box 13407, Austin, TX 78711.

94. *A Coastal Homeowner's Guide to Floodproofing*, by the Massachusetts Disaster Recovery Team. This booklet combines a checklist to take the homeowner through the process of flood-proofing existing houses with tips on dealing with engineers and contractors. Available from the Office of the Lieutenant Governor, State House, Boston, MA 02133.

95. *Estimating Increased Building Costs Resulting from Use of a Hurricane-Resistant Building Code*. Should be of interest to builders of new structures. Available from the Texas Coastal and Marine Council, P.O. Box 13407, Austin, TX 78711

96. *Structural Failures: Modes, Causes, Responsibilities*, 1973. See especially the chapter "Failure of Structures Due to Extreme Winds," pp. 49–77. Available from the Research Council on Performance of Structures, American Society of Civil Engineers, 345 East 47th Street, New York, NY 10017.

97. *Wind-Resistant Design Concepts for Residences*, by Delbart B. Ward. Displays construction problems with vivid sketches, illustrations, and methods of tying structures down. Considerable text and excellent illustrations devoted to methods of strengthening residences. Offers recommendations for relatively inexpensive modifications that will increase the safety of residences subject to severe winds. Chapter 8, "How to Calculate Wind Forces and Design Wind-Resistant Structures," should be of particular interest to the designer. Available as TR-83 from the Civil Defense Preparedness Agency, Department of Defense, Washington, DC 20301; or the Civil Defense Preparedness Agency, 2800 Eastern Boulevard, Baltimore, MD 21220.

98. *Interim Guidelines for Building Occupant Protection from Tornadoes and Extreme Winds*, TR-83A, and *Tornado Protection—Selecting and Designing Safe Areas in a Building*, TR-83B. These are supplement publications to entry 97 and are available at the same address.

99. *Hurricane-Resistant Construction for Homes*, by T. L. Walton, Jr., 1976. A good summary of hurricanes, storm surge, damage assessment, and guidelines for hurricane-resistant construction. The booklet presents technical concepts on probability and its implications on home design in hazard areas. There is also a brief summary of federal and local guidelines. Available from Florida Sea Grant Publications, Florida Cooperative Extension Service, Marine Advisory Program, Coastal Engineering Laboratory, University of Florida, Gainesville, FL 32611.

Wood structures

100. *Houses Can Resist Hurricanes*, by the U.S. Forest Service, 1965. An excellent paper with numerous details on construction in general. Pole house construction is treated in particular detail (pp. 29–45). Available as Research Paper FPL 33 from Forest Products Laboratory, Forest Service, U.S. Department of Agriculture, P.O. Box 5130, Madison, WI 53705.

101. *Wood Structures Survive Hurricane Camille's Winds*. Available as Research Paper FPL 123, October 1969, from Forest Products Laboratory, Forest Service, U.S. Department of Agriculture, P.O. Box 5130, Madison, WI 53705.

102. "Wood Structures Can Resist Hurricanes," by Gerald E. Sherward, in *Civil Engineering* magazine, September 1972, pp. 91–94. Available from most university libraries.

Masonry construction

103. *Standard Details for One-Story Concrete Block Residences*, by the Masonry Institute of America. Contains nine fold-out drawings that illustrate the details of constructing a concrete block house. It presents principles of reinforcement and good connections that are aimed at design for seismic zones, but these apply to design in hurricane zones as well. Written for both layman and designer. Available as publication 701 from Masonry Institute of America, 2550 Beverly Boulevard, Los Angeles, CA 90057.

104. *Masonry Design Manual*, by the Masonry Institute of America. A very comprehensive manual that covers all types of masonry including brick, concrete block, glazed structural units, stone, and veneer. This book is probably of more interest to the designer than to the layman. Available as publication 601 from the Masonry Institute of America, 2550 Beverly Boulevard, Los Angeles, CA 90057.

Pole house construction

105. *Pole House Construction*. Available from the American Wood Preservers Institute, 1651 Old Meadows Road, McLean, VA 22101.

106. *Elevated Residential Structures*, prepared by the American Institute of Architects Foundation (1735 New York Avenue, N.W., Washington, DC 20006) for the Federal Emergency Management Agency, 1984. This excellent publication outlines coastal and riverine flood hazards and the necessity for proper planning and construction. The 137-page book discusses the National Flood Insurance Program, site analysis and design, design examples and construction techniques including illustrations, glossary, references, and worksheets for estimating building costs. Available from the Superintendent of Documents, U.S. Government Printing Office, Washington, DC 20402 (request stock no. 1984 0-438-116), or contact FEMA Region I Office, J. W. McCormack Post Office and Courthouse Building, Room 442, Boston, MA 02109 (phone: [617] 223-4741), and request FEMA publication no. 54.

Mobile homes

107. *Protecting Mobile Homes from High Winds*, TR-75, by the Civil Defense Preparedness Agency, 1974. An excellent 16-page booklet that outlines methods of tying down mobile homes and means of protection such as positioning and windbreaks. Publication 1974-0-537-785, available free from the Superintendent of Documents, U.S. Government Printing Office, Washington, DC 20402, or from the U.S. Army, AG Publications Center, Civil Defense Branch, 2800 Eastern Boulevard (Middle River), Baltimore, MD 21220.

108. *Suggested Technical Requirements for Mobile Home Tie Down Ordinances*, TR-73-1, prepared by the Civil Defense Preparedness Agency, July 1974. Should be used in conjunction with TR-75 noted above (entry 107). Available from the U.S. Army Publications Center, Civil Defense Branch, 2800 Eastern Boulevard (Middle River), Baltimore, MD 21220.

109. The Living with the Shore series includes the following additional titles:

The Beaches Are Moving: The Drowning of America's Shoreline
From Currituck to Calabash: Living with North Carolina's Barrier Islands
Living with the Alabama/Mississippi Shore
Living with the California Coast
Living with Chesapeake Bay and Virginia's Ocean Shores
Living with the East Florida Shore
Living with the Lake Erie Shore
Living with Long Island's South Shore
Living with the Louisiana Shore
Living with the New Jersey Shore
Living with the Shore of Puget Sound and the Georgia Strait
Living with the South Carolina Shore
Living with the Texas Shore
Living with the West Florida Shore

Available through your local bookstore, or order from Duke University Press, 6697 College Station, Durham, NC 27708.

Index

About the Authors

Joseph and Alice Kelley are professional geologists and residents of the state of Maine. Orrin H. Pilkey, Sr., is a retired civil engineer.
